THE LAW OF SPEECH AND THE FIRST AMENDMENT

by

Margaret C. Jasper, Esq.

Oceana's Legal Almanac Series:
Law for the Layperson

1999
Oceana Publications, Inc.
Dobbs Ferry, N.Y.

#41488700

Information contained in this work has been obtained by Oceana Publications from sources believed to be reliable. However, neither the Publisher nor its authors guarantee the accuracy or completeness of any information published herein, and neither Oceana nor its authors shall be responsible for any errors, omissions or damages arising from the use of this information. This work is published with the understanding that Oceana and its authors are supplying information, but are not attempting to render legal or other professional services. If such services are required, the assistance of an appropriate professional should be sought.

You may order this or any other Oceana publications by visiting Oceana's Web Site at http://www.oceanalaw.com

Library of Congress Cataloging-in-Publication Data

Jasper, Margaret C.
　　The law of speech and the First Amendment / by
Margaret C. Jasper.
　　　　p. cm.—(Oceana's legal almanac series. Law for the layperson)
　　Includes bibliographical references.
　　ISBN 0-379-11335-X (clothbound : alk. paper)
　　1. Freedom of speech—United States—Popular works.
　　2. Freedom of the press—United States—Popular works.
　　I. Title. II. Series.
　　KF4772.Z9 J37 1999
　　342.73'0853—dc21
　　　　　　　　　　　　　　　　　　　　　　99-32743
　　　　　　　　　　　　　　　　　　　　　　CIP

Oceana's Legal Almanac Series: Law for the Layperson
ISSN 1075-7376

To My Husband Chris

Your love and support
are my motivation and inspiration

-and-

In memory of my son, Jimmy

Other Volumes Available in the Series

For more information or to order call: 1-914-693-8100
or visit us at www.oceanalaw.com

ABOUT THE AUTHOR

MARGARET C. JASPER is an attorney engaged in the general practice of law in South Salem, New York, concentrating in the areas of personal injury and entertainment law. Ms. Jasper holds a Juris Doctor degree from Pace University School of Law, White Plains, New York, is a member of the New York and Connecticut bars, and is certified to practice before the United States District Courts for the Southern and Eastern Districts of New York, and the United States Supreme Court. Ms. Jasper has been appointed to the panel of arbitrators of the American Arbitration Association and the law guardian panel for the Family Court of the State of New York, is a member of the Association of Trial Lawyers of America, and is a New York State licensed real estate broker and member of the Westchester County Board of Realtors, operating as Jasper Real Estate, in South Salem, New York.

Ms. Jasper is the author and general editor of the following legal almanacs: Juvenile Justice and Children's Law; Marriage and Divorce; Estate Planning; The Law of Contracts; The Law of Dispute Resolution; Law for the Small Business Owner; The Law of Personal Injury; Real Estate Law for the Homeowner and Broker; Everyday Legal Forms; Dictionary of Selected Legal Terms; The Law of Medical Malpractice; The Law of Product Liability; The Law of No-Fault Insurance; The Law of Immigration; The Law of Libel and Slander; The Law of Buying and Selling; Elder Law; The Right to Die; AIDS Law; The Law of Obscenity and Pornography; The Law of Child Custody; The Law of Debt Collection; Consumer Rights Law; Bankruptcy Law for the Individual Debtor; Victim's Rights Law; Animal Rights Law; Workers' Compensation Law; Employee Rights in the Workplace; Probate Law; Environmental Law; Labor Law; The Americans with Disabilities Act; The Law of Capital Punishment; Education Law; The Law of Violence Against Women; Landlord-Tenant Law; Insurance Law; Religion and the Law; Commercial Law; Motor Vehicle Law; Social Security Law and the Law of Drunk Driving.

TABLE OF CONTENTS

INTRODUCTION

The simple constitutional language setting forth the First Amendment guarantees of expression—freedom of speech and the press—has been the subject of many a debate. There are a number of differing views concerning the scope of this provision as intended by the original framers of the Constitution. Some argue that its applicability in a particular situation largely depends on circumstances existing at the time. Some hold the belief that the freedom was intended to apply only to political speech. Others argue that there should be no restrictions placed on speech in a free society whatsoever.

Neither has the Supreme Court developed any concrete test on how and when this constitutional guarantee should be applied in a given case, thus case law continues to evolve and interpretations change. Nevertheless, there is a commonly held belief that freedom of expression is essential to the proper administration of a free society and necessary to the "marketplace of ideas."

The fact that freedom of speech is the "first freedom" mentioned in the First Amendment demonstrates that the framers of the Constitution held this right in high regard and believed that freedom of inquiry and liberty of expression were the hallmarks of a democratic society. Nevertheless, throughout history, there have been times when First Amendment rights have come under heavy attack. For example, during the infamous "McCarthy" era, numerous lives and careers were ruined when individuals espousing a certain political viewpoint—and those believed to associate with such individuals—were blacklisted.

Many believe that the First Amendment freedoms are presently under attack by the government seeking to regulate the internet, music lyrics and other forms of art and entertainment, which are viewed as predominant factors in the "downfall" of morals and the increase in youth violence in the United States. They argue that the very purpose of the First Amendment is to protect the most controversial speech from such government suppression and regulation. Others argue that the framers of the Constitution were intent on protecting political speech, not every form of explicit or offensive expression now claiming constitutional protection.

Nevrtheless, the simple language of the First Amendment leaves much to interpretation. Thus, the Supreme Court has been called on to set standards and guidelines to resolve these disputes. As a result of the many struggles over protecting First Amendment rights, free expression in the United States receives more protection than any other country in the world.

This almanac discusses the background and adoption of the First Amendment guarantees of free expression. It also examines the manner in which the Supreme Court has applied the doctrine in a variety of cases, and the standards which have evolved. First Amendment issues concerning expressive conduct, public education, arts and entertainment, obscenity, cyberspace, and commercial speech, and the manner in which the government has tried to regulate and censor these various channels, are also explored.

The Appendices provide resource directories, relevant statutes, and other pertinent information and data. The Glossary contains definitions of many of the terms used throughout the almanac.

CHAPTER 1:

HISTORICAL BACKGROUND

Drafting and Ratification of the First Amendment

Agreement on the final wording of the First Amendment to the United States Constitution required compromise between libertarians, such as James Madison, and more conservative representatives, such as Alexander Hamilton. Hamilton and his cohorts believed that the English common law provided adequate free speech protection. However, Madison adamantly argued that freedom of the press and rights of conscience were unguarded in the British constitution. Thus, in 1789, Madison introduced his version of the free speech and press clause to the House of Representatives. It provided:

> The people shall not be deprived or abridged of their right to speak, to write, or to publish their sentiments; and the freedom of the press, as one of the great bulwarks of liberty, shall be inviolable.

Madison's language was rewritten by the House Committee to provide:

> The freedom of speech and of the press, and the right of the people peaceably to assemble and consult for their common good, and to apply to the Government for redress of grievances, shall not be infringed.

The clause then went to the Senate, which rewrote the provision as follows:

> That Congress shall make no law abridging the freedom of speech, or of the press, or the right of the people peaceably to assemble and consult for their common good, and to petition the government for a redress of grievances.

Subsequently, the religion clauses and free speech and press clauses were combined by the Senate, and the language of the First Amendment was finalized:

> Congress shall make no law respecting an establishment of religion, or prohibiting the free exercise thereof; or abridging the freedom of speech, or of the press; or the right of the people peaceably to assemble, and to petition the government for a redress of grievances.

The Bill of Rights was added to the United States Constitution in December 1791, after being ratified by the required three fourths of the states.

Framers' Intent

There was no recorded debate in the Senate concerning the meaning given to the speech and press clauses of the First Amendment, nor was there any meaningful debate in the House of Representatives. Notably, Madison's concern was that the propositions were stated concisely so as to encourage ratification. Thus, the simplicity of the principles embodied in the First Amendment have led to much controversy concerning their interpretation.

It is no question that the framers believed freedom of speech and of the press was essential to the establishment of a free society. It is also widely held that the drafters adopted the Blackstonian view when ratifying the First Amendment. William Blackstone was an English jurist regarded by the framers as the preeminent authority on the common law. His view concerning freedom of expression was that there should be no prior restraints placed on the liberties of speech or publication, but that anyone publishing "improper, mischievous, or illegal" speech could subsequently be punished.

Thomas Jefferson is known to have held the Blackstonian view and, in fact, advised Madison that "a declaration that the federal government will never restrain the presses from printing anything they please . . . will not take away the liability of the printers for false facts printed." In support of his view, Jefferson suggested the following First Amendment language:

> The people shall not be deprived or abridged of their right to speak, to write or otherwise to publish anything *but false facts* affecting injuriously the life, liberty, property, or reputation of others or affecting the peace of the confederacy with foreign nations.

While the final wording of the First Amendment embodied the common law view that freedom of speech was protected against prior restraint by the government, it gave no explicit protection from punishment for what one might print, such as statements which may be libelous, defamatory, or seditious. Indeed, the following three forms of criminal libel which had existed in England were, in fact, adopted by the colonies as part of their own criminal law:

1. Obscene libel was *per se* sanctionable even if the statement was true.

2. Blasphemous libel against religious beliefs was illegal even if true.

3. Seditious libel against the government was outlawed.

Applicability to the States

Madison had originally proposed First Amendment language that would limit the power of the states in suppressing speech, including a guarantee of freedom of the press. Although this language passed in the House, it was defeated by the Senate.

Nevertheless, the Supreme Court subsequently held that the Fourteenth Amendment made the First Amendment prohibitions applicable to the states, and restrained the power of the states to suppress speech and the press. For example, in Stromberg v. California, 283 U.S. 359 (1931), a state statute was voided on grounds of its interference with free speech.

The Supreme Court also held that state common law was subject to the First Amendment. In *Bridges v. California*, 314 U.S. 252 (1941), contempt convictions of a newspaper editor and his staff for publishing commentary on pending cases was overturned. Justice Black opined that the First Amendment enlarged protections for speech, press, and religion beyond those enjoyed under English common law.

In 1969, in *Brandenburg v. Ohio*, 395 U.S. 444 (1969), the Supreme Court further elaborated on a state's right to infringe on free speech and press, holding that these constitutional guarantees "do not permit a state to forbid or proscribe advocacy of the use of force . . . except where such advocacy is directed to inciting or producing imminent lawless action and is likely to incite or produce such action."

CHAPTER 2:

OVERVIEW OF THE FIRST AMENDMENT

In General

The First Amendment protects the right to freedom of religion and freedom of expression from government interference. Freedom of expression is made up of the rights of freedom of speech; press; assembly; the right to petition the government for a redress of grievances; and the implied right of association and belief.

The text of the First Amendment is set forth at Appendix 1.

The Supreme Court, responsible for interpreting the scope of the protection afforded these rights, has stated that freedom of expression is "the matrix, the indispensable condition of nearly every other form of freedom."

Although the First Amendment is only expressly applicable to Congress, it has been interpreted by the Court as applying to the entire federal government. Furthermore, as previously stated, the Court has interpreted the due process clause of the Fourteenth Amendment as protecting the rights in the First Amendment from interference by state governments.

The text of the Fourteenth Amendment is set forth at Appendix 2.

The role of the freedom of expression clauses has been to protect those who wish to freely publish matters of public concern, and openly criticize the official conduct of public authorities, without fear of governmental retribution. There are a number of organizations, such as the American Civil Liberties Union (ACLU), that vigorously protect free expression. They are vigilant of proposed legislation that seeks to threaten any of the rights contained in the First Amendment, and are quick to intervene.

A directory of organizations concerned with First Amendment issues is set forth at Appendix 3.

Freedom of Speech

The foremost right included in the term "freedom of expression" is freedom of speech—the right to express oneself without interference or constraint by the government. This right is not restricted to the spoken word but encompasses other mediums of expression that communicate information—known generally as "symbolic speech." Protected expression may include wearing symbols, such as "AIDS" ribbons and political buttons;

music lyrics; wearing slogans on t-shirts; and participating in sit-ins and marches.

As more fully discussed in this almanac, the Supreme Court requires the government to provide substantial justification if it attempts to interfere with freedom of speech or regulate the content of speech. Nevertheless, the Supreme Court has recognized that the government has the right to prohibit some speech that may cause a breach of the peace or cause violence.

Freedom of the Press

The constitutional guarantee of freedom of the press is similar to the right of freedom of speech, and is also included in the term "freedom of expression." Freedom of the press allows for expression through publication and dissemination. However, this has led to some debate over whether freedom of the press grants greater protection to the so-called "institutional press" over other individuals or groups.

In Houchins v. KQED, 438 U.S. 1 (1978), Justice Stewart expressed the Court's view on the issue:

"That the First Amendment speaks separately of freedom of speech and freedom of the press is no constitutional accident, but an acknowledgment of the critical role played by the press in American society. The Constitution requires sensitivity to that role, and to the special needs of the press in performing it effectively."

However, Chief Justice Burger declined to adopt this view, stating that the institutional press had no special privilege:

"The Court has not yet squarely resolved whether the press clause confers upon the institutional press any freedom from government restraint not enjoyed by all others."

Subsequent Supreme Court decisions appear to concur with Chief Justice Burger's view that the press clause does not confer any particular power on the press than that given to the general public, although some also maintain the view that the role of the press in disseminating news and information to the public may yet entitle it to some deference not enjoyed by all. Nevertheless, the scope of that deference has not in any way been delineated by the Court.

Right of Assembly

The right to assemble allows people to gather for peaceful and lawful purposes. This constitutional right, however, is limited to the right to associate for First Amendment purposes. It does not include a right of "social association." For example, the government may prohibit people from associating in groups that engage in or promote illegal activities.

Right to Petition the Government

The right to petition the government for a redress of grievances guarantees people the right to request relief from the government to correct some type of wrong or injustice. This may include taking formal legal action. This constitutional guarantee goes hand in hand with the right of assembly to allow people to join together to seek change from the government.

Content Neutral Restrictions on Speech

The Government is permitted to limit some protected speech by placing restrictions on the *time, place and manner* of the speech. Laws regulating the time, place and manner of speech are common and routinely upheld provided they meet the following conditions:

Content Neutral

The law must be content-neutral. The government cannot engage in "viewpoint discrimination." For example, the government can require a group to obtain a permit to hold a demonstration. However, it cannot deny a permit based on the content of the proposed speech.

Thus, an ordinance barring picketing "within 50 feet of a foreign embassy *if the picket signs cast insult' on the foreign government"* would not be constitutionally valid because it is not merely a time/place/manner restriction, but attempts to regulate the content of speech.

In addition, if a demonstration or rally turns from mere speech to certain types of action, the government may be permitted to intervene. For example, although demonstrators are permitted to picket an establishment, they do not have the right to block entrances and otherwise harass people. The government can shut down speech wherever it would be disruptive and inappropriate so long as the restraint is content neutral.

Neutral As Applied

The law must be neutral on its face and as applied. This means that there can be no executive discretion. If a law gives some executive officer the ability to permit or ban certain speech, it will generally be struck down because it is likely to result in content-based discrimination.

Substantial Opportunity

The law must allow *substantial other opportunities* for the speech to take place. For example, an ordinance that provides there can be no amplified speech between the hours of 11:00 p.m. and 7:00 a.m. in residential areas is constitutionally valid as a time, place and manner restriction.

Content-Based Restrictions on Speech

The Government adopts and enforces many measures which are designed to further a valid interest but which may have restrictive effects upon freedom of expression. In general, the government may not regulate speech because of its message, its ideas, its subject matter, or its content. Most content-based restrictions on speech are struck down as unconstitutional. They require a *compelling governmental interest* and a statute that is narrowly drawn to be upheld.

In *Chaplinsky v. New Hampshire*, 315 U.S. 568 (1942), in deciding what types of speech are not protected under the First Amendment, the Court opined that "certain well-defined and narrowly limited classes of speech ... are no essential part of any exposition of ideas, and are of such slight social value as a step to truth" that the government may prevent those utterances and punish those uttering them without raising any constitutional problems.

Thus, as more fully discussed below, government regulation of expression may occur in a number of contexts:

Arts and Entertainment

Sexual expression in the arts and entertainment fields has always been a target by groups wishing to censor the content of music lyrics, television programming, movies and the theater. Proponents of censorship argue that violence and immorality among the nation's youth correlates with the images children are exposed to through the media.

Government censorship in the arts and entertainment is more fully discussed in Chapter 8 of this almanac.

Commercial Speech

Commercial speech is entitled to First Amendment protection, however, the Supreme Court has clearly held that there are differences between commercial speech and other forms of expression which subject it to a different degree of protection.

Basically, commercial speech must be allowed if it is truthful and informational. An advertisement may be suppressed if it is misleading or if it pertains to an illegal product. If the advertisement is not misleading and the product is not unlawful, commercial speech can be suppressed only if there is a *substantial state interest*. Further, the degree of suppression can be no more than necessary. In making this determination, the Supreme Court has established a four-prong test:

1. Commercial speech which does not accurately inform the public about lawful activity is not entitled to protection and can be suppressed.

2. If commercial speech is protected, a state seeking to regulate or limit the speech must assert a substantial interest to be achieved by its restriction.

3. If the state's restriction provides only ineffective or remote support for the asserted purpose, the restriction cannot be sustained.

4. If the state's interest could be similarly served by a more limited restriction on commercial speech, the excessive restriction will not be upheld.

Thus, the degree of protection afforded commercial speech differs from other types of protected speech in that the government does not have to endure inaccuracies and may require commercial speech to contain additional information, such as warnings or disclaimers, in order to ensure that its content is not deceptive.

Defamatory Falsehoods and Actual Malice

In general, defamatory speech is not protected under the First Amendment and is punishable. Defamatory speech may be either slanderous, which refers to spoken defamation, or libelous, which is printed defamation. Nevertheless, as set forth below, Supreme Court has held that when a defamatory statement involves a public official, *actual malice* must be proven.

New York Times Co. v. Sullivan

The landmark case of *New York Times Co. v. Sullivan*, 376 U.S. 254 (1964), stood for the proposition that defamatory falsehoods about public officials can only be punished if the offended official is able to prove that the falsehoods were published with "actual malice,"—i.e., with knowledge that the statement was false or with reckless disregard of whether it was false or not.

In this case, The New York Times had published a paid advertisement by a civil rights organization criticizing the response of a Southern community to demonstrations led by Dr. Martin Luther King. The advertisement contained several factual errors. The plaintiff, a city commissioner in charge of the police department, claimed that the advertisement had libeled him even though he was not referred to by name or title and even though several of the incidents described had occurred prior to his taking office. The lower court found for the plaintiff.

Unanimously, the Supreme Court reversed the lower court's judgment. The plaintiff argued that the First Amendment did not protect libelous publications. Nevertheless, in reaching its decision, the court held:

"[Libel] must be measured by standards that satisfy the First Amendment . . . [W]e consider this case against the background of a profound national commitment to the principle that debate on public issues should be uninhibited, robust, and wide-open, and that it may well include vehement, caustic, and sometimes unpleasantly sharp attacks on government and public officials . . . Error is inevitable in any free debate and to place liability upon that score, and especially to place on the speaker the burden of proving truth, would introduce self- censorship and stifle the free expression which the First Amendment protects . . . The constitutional guarantees require, we think, a federal rule that prohibits a public official from recovering damages for a defamatory falsehood relating to his official conduct unless he proves that the statement was made with *actual malice*, that is, with knowledge that it was false or with reckless disregard of whether it was false or not."

Hate Speech

The right to engage in "hate speech" is a hotly contested topic. Advocates for free speech argue that the First Amendment protects all speech, regardless of whether it is offensive because any infringement of free speech rights will endanger the rights of all people.

The issue of hate speech is more fully discussed in Chapters 10 of this almanac.

Internet

In recent years, the internet has been a target of the censorship campaign. There is much concern that on-line speech is harmful to children. Thus, a number of bills have been proposed in order to screen and filter the content of speech over the internet, and to further protect children who use the internet.

The issue of internet regulation is more fully discussed in Chapter 8 of this almanac.

National Security Matters

The Supreme Court has recognized a limited right of the government to keep certain national security matters secret. For example, during time of war, troop deployments could be censored. Historically, the government has attempted to use "national security" to try and shield itself from criticism. However, the Court has never upheld an injunction against speech on national security grounds.

The issue of government regulation of speech on national security grounds is more fully discussed in Chapter 4 of this almanac.

Obscenity

Material which is deemed "obscene" is not afforded protection under the First Amendment. However, the definition of obscenity has been narrowly construed. In general, to be considered obscene, the obscenity must: (i) appeal to the prurient interest; (ii) be patently offensive to the average person in society; and (iii) lack serious value.

Government restrictions of obscenity are more fully discussed in Chapter 7 of this almanac.

Seditious Speech

Opposing the government through speech has been subject to punishment throughout much of American history under laws proscribing seditious utterances. The validity of these laws were continually attacked on First Amendment grounds because of the restriction they imposed upon criticism of government and public officials.

The history of government regulation of seditious speech and advocacy are more fully discussed in Chapter 4 of this almanac.

Legislative Investigations

Legislative investigations conducted by congressional and state legislative committees in order to develop information to form a basis for proposed legislation is subject to some uncertain limitations when they result in deterrence or sanction of protected beliefs, associations and conduct.

The Court initially took the position that legislative inquiries would be closely scrutinized for First Amendment violations. However, in subsequent cases, the Court upheld a wide range of legislative investigations, applying a balancing of interests test — i.e., balancing the legislative interest in inquiring about both protected and unprotected associations and conduct, against limited restraints upon the speech and association rights of witnesses

In more recent cases, the Court reformulated this balancing of interests test, and has required that the investigating committee show "a subordinating interest which is compelling" to justify the restraint on First Amendment rights resulting from the inquiry.

Miscellaneous Constitutional Standards

Over the years, the Supreme Court has developed certain general constitutional standards or tests which are also applicable to the First Amendment, including the following:

Vagueness

The "vagueness" doctrine generally requires that a law be precise enough to give fair warning to individuals that certain conduct is criminal, and provide adequate standards to enforcement agencies, factfinders, and reviewing courts. If the law does not give clear notice of what is prohibited, it violates due process.

Although this provision is applicable to any criminal and many civil statutes, it applies to the First Amendment because it is also concerned that protected conduct will be deterred out of fear that a particular law may apply. In fact, vagueness has been the basis for voiding a number of statutes, including obscenity laws, public demonstration prohibitions, and loyalty oath requirements.

Overbreadth

If a law burdens more speech than is necessary for a compelling interest, it violates the First Amendment. Because there is a need for precision in drafting any law that affects First Amendment rights, any statute which is "overbroad," encompassing protected and unprotected speech and conduct, will generally be struck down as unconstitutional. In resolving a non-First Amendment issue, the Court may simply void the statute's application to the protected speech and/or conduct.

Least Restrictive Means

The Supreme Court has held that when a government endeavors to carry out a particular goal, and it has a variety of means to reach that goal, the government must use the measure that least interferes with an individual's First Amendment Rights. This is generally known as using the "least restrictive means necessary." In addition, the chosen measure must relate to achievement of the goal in order to be justified.

CHAPTER 3:

PRIOR RESTRAINT DOCTRINE

In General

Prior restraint refers to legal action seeking to suppress speech prior to its expression, rather than assess punishment on the basis of its content. For example, under this doctrine, a newspaper can be prohibited by the Government from printing certain information which the newspapers wishes to print.

Prior restraint is a doctrine which is especially disfavored and rarely upheld by the Court. Subsequent punishment is ordinarily the manner in which unprotected speech is remedied. Prior restraint requires a significant cause and a prompt judicial determination that the restraint was justified.

The English Licensing System

In the 16th century, Henry VIII placed the entire press under a "licensing" system. Under the English licensing system, all newspapers, printing presses and printers were licensed and nothing could be published without prior approval of the state or church authorities. Editors could be imprisoned for printing libel about the government.

Throughout the Tudor and Stuart periods, the primary function of the detested Star Chamber was censorship of books. Offenders were sentenced to long prison terms, were heavily fined, and subjected to extremely cruel and inhuman punishments. The Star Chamber was finally abolished by Parliament in 1641 and censorship was lifted.

Following the abolition of the Star Chamber and censorship, Parliament became alarmed when "scandalous, seditious and libelous" publications began to appear in the news. Thus, Parliament passed a new censorship act, under which unlicensed printing was also banned. The new act was modeled after the old Star Chamber practices, however, the censors were appointed by Parliament. Control of the presses continued for the next fifty years, until 1689, when William and Mary acceded to the throne and became more tolerant of the press. The English licensing system finally ended in 1695 following a long struggle.

The Prior Restraint Doctrine in America

The English licensing system of prior restraint never took hold in American jurisprudence. In fact, a fundamental principle of the freedom of expression guarantees is the *immunity* from previous restraints or censorship. The Supreme Court has generally held that prior restraints violate the First Amendment. In Bantam Books v. Sullivan, 372 U.S. 58 (1963), the Court stated that "[a]ny system of prior restraints of expression comes to this Court bearing a heavy presumption against its constitutional validity."

New York Times Co. v. United States

New York Times Co. v. United States, 403 U.S. 713 (1971)—a case commonly known as the *Pentagon Papers* case—is a well-known prior restraints case in which the Supreme Court rejected the government's attempt at prior restraint of a classified Pentagon study of the Vietnam War.

Dr. Daniel Ellsberg, a Pentagon official, provided top secret government information concerning Vietnam to the newspapers. The information was voluminous and, although it did not provide any military secrets or tactical information, it was embarrassing to U.S. Government officials because the information revealed that they had misled and manipulated foreign governments. The New York Times and the Washington Post published two articles using excerpts from the document.

Although the government couldn't do anything to retrieve what had already been published, they didn't know how much more information had been leaked, thus, they petitioned the Federal Appeals Court for a restraining order on all information not yet revealed. Their basis for the petition was that the information was a matter of national security, and the restraining order was granted.

The case was appealed to the U.S. Supreme Court. The newspapers claimed it had a First Amendment right to print the document, which they said contained no secret information. The Nixon administration claimed that its publication would harm the national interest. Nevertheless, the Court found that the government had not sufficiently justified its request for prior restraint, and permitted both newspapers to proceed with publication.

Although the majority arrived at the same conclusion, they based their decisions on different reasoning. Most of the Justices held that the Government has the right to restrain information, but that it must meet a high standard of proof—i.e., it must be able to prove that the information would "surely" result in "direct, immediate, and irreparable harm" to the nation. The Government was unable to meet its burden in the *Pentagon Papers* case. The fear of "embarrassment" to Government officials was held not to be a perilous consequence of publication.

Justices Douglas and Black simply held that prior restraint is anathema and to restrain the press would undermine the First Amendment. Justice Douglas opined:

"I believe that every moment's continuance of the injunctions against these newspapers amounts to a flagrant, indefensible and continuing violation of the First Amendment . . . "

Constitutional Prior Restraint by Government

Despite the holding in the *Pentagon Papers* case, the principle of immunity from prior restraint is not absolute, and prior restraint may be constitutional under certain circumstances:

Prior Restraint in National Security Matters

The Supreme Court has upheld prior restraint in connection with certain national security matters where the government is able to meet its burden of "irreparable harm." For example, the government may be able to restrain a publication from publishing military secrets, such as troop movements during wartime. Government regulation in national security matters is more fully discussed in Chapter 4.

Protection of Certain Individuals and Groups

The government may be permitted to restrain a publication from publishing information the government does not want printed in order to protect an individual or group, such as rape victims or informants. However, if the information happens to leak out, the press is then free to print it.

Classified Information

Under the Classified Information Procedure Act (CIPA), a judge determines whether certain documents sought to be classified as secret by the government are properly classified as such. Secret court opinions are only available with FBI clearance.

The Right to a Fair Trial and the Issuance of Gag Orders

In *Nebraska Press Association v. Stuart*, 427 U.S. 539 (1976), the Supreme Court unanimously set aside a state court injunction barring the publication of information that might prejudice the subsequent trial of a criminal defendant. In determining whether "gag orders" were ever permissible, a "clear and present danger" test was formulated which considered the following factors in deciding whether to impose a restraint on press reporters:

1. The nature and extent of pretrial news coverage;

2. Whether other measures were likely to mitigate the harm; and

3. How effectively a restraining order would operate to prevent the threatened danger.

Applying these three tests to the facts of the case, the Chief Justice agreed that:

1. There was intense and pervasive pretrial publicity and more could be expected; but that

2. The lower courts had made little effort to assess the prospects of other methods of preventing or mitigating the effects of such publicity; and that

3. In any event, the restraining order was unlikely to have the desired effect of protecting the defendant's rights.

The Court further proposed that any party seeking a restraining order would have a heavy burden to meet to justify the action—a showing that without a prior restraint a fair trial would be denied. Nevertheless, Justice Brennan, in his concurrence, rejected the notion that restraining orders were ever permissible unless national harm would result from publication, and further opined that:

"[T]here can be no prohibition on the publication by the press of any information pertaining to pending judicial proceedings or the operation of the criminal justice system . . . because the trial court could adequately protect a defendant's right to a fair trial through other means, even if there were conflict of constitutional rights, the possibility of damage to the fair trial right would be so speculative that the burden of justification could not be met."

While this case did not foreclose the possibility of a "gag order," it did limit the number that could successfully be obtained, and focused more on finding alternatives to protect the right to a fair trial, such as banning communication concerning trial issues between the press and the prosecution, defense attorneys, law enforcement officials, and court officers.

In *Seattle Times Co. v. Rhinehart*, however, an order restraining the press, as a party litigant, from disseminating information obtained during pre-trial discovery, was upheld. The Court held that such orders protecting parties from abuses of discovery require no heightened First Amendment scrutiny.

Prior Restraint of Obscenity

As the following cases demonstrate, obscenity is one area that has not enjoyed the same level of protection against prior restraint generally afforded under the First Amendment.

Kingsley Books v. Brown

In *Kingsley Books v. Brown*, 354 U.S. 436 (1957), the Court upheld a state statute which, although it appeared to have some characteristics of prior restraint, in actuality its restraining effect was no more than that of a criminal statute since the penalties only applied after publication.

Times Film Corp. v. City of Chicago

In *Times Film Corp. v. City of Chicago*, 365 U.S. 43 (1961), a divided Court specifically affirmed that, at least in the case of motion pictures, the First Amendment did not prevent a Board of Censors from devising a licensing system under which they could refuse to license a film for public exhibition if it was found to be obscene.

Subsequent Punishment

Although the issue of prior restraint of speech has been of utmost concern, much of First Amendment case law has addressed the problem of subsequent punishment. The two principles go hand in hand for what good is it to have the freedom to express one's thoughts yet face prosecution after having done so. The concern is that this would inevitably lead to self-censorship by those who feared criminal or civil liability even if their utterances were truthful.

CHAPTER 4:

GOVERNMENT REGULATION OF SEDITIOUS SPEECH AND ADVOCACY

In General

The government is obligated to provide for the security of the nation and protect it from its enemies, both foreign and domestic. As a means to meeting this obligation, government officials have, at times, infringed upon the First Amendment guarantees of free speech and press.

Following the passage of the First Amendment, as further set forth below, a number of federal and state laws were passed which sought to restrain certain types of seditious speech and advocacy. In a number of cases, the Supreme Court was called upon to determine whether or not the government overstepped its bounds.

The Alien and Sedition Act of 1798

One of the most harmful attacks on freedom of expression came with the passage of the infamous Alien and Sedition Act of 1798 during the French and Indian War. The Act sought to limit First Amendment guarantees by preventing the publication of false or malicious information concerning the government. The Act had full support of the Federalists, who were fearful of the threat of foreign ideas and their subversive tendencies. Under the Act, punishment would be assessed against those who would:

> "[w]rite, print, utter or publish . . . any false, scandalous and malicious writing or writings against the government of the United States, or either house of the Congress of the United States, or the President of the United States, with intent to defame the said government, or either house of the said Congress, or the said President, or to bring them, or either of them, into contempt or disrepute."

Much debate followed concerning the constitutionality of the Alien and Sedition Act insofar as its restraint of criticism against the government and public officials appeared inconsistent with, and outlawed by, the First Amendment. The Act was used by the prevailing Federalist Party to prosecute prominent Republican newspaper editors during the late 18th century. During the 19th century, sedition, criminal anarchy and criminal conspiracy laws were used to suppress the speech of abolitionists, religious minorities, suffragists, labor organizers, and pacifists.

The Espionage Act of 1917

The early 20th century continued the assault on freedom of expression. Union meetings were banned and courts routinely granted injunctions prohibiting strikes and other labor protests. Many people were arrested or blacklisted merely for their membership in certain groups, or for their association with individuals regarded as radical by the government.

During World War I, the United States government feared sabotage and espionage, and felt the need to suppress people who might undermine the war effort. In fact, even peaceful protesters opposed to World War I were sent to prison. In response, Congress enacted the Espionage Act of 1917.

People arrested under the Act tended to be socialists; activists; Bolsheviks and some Pacifists. There was a general indictment framed for the perpetrator which consisted of "uttering . . . disseminating literature . . . which is anti-draft . . . advocated cause of enemies, etc." This was a lesser offense of treason which, unlike treason, also governed non-citizens.

Schenck v. United States

In *Schenck v. United States*, 249 U.S. 47 (1919), the first post-World War I case to reach the Supreme Court, a conviction under the Espionage Act was upheld where the defendant allegedly attempted to cause insubordination among the military by the circulation of leaflets denouncing the draft.

The defendant, Charles Schenck, was a member of the Philadelphia Socialist Party. He mailed leaflets to men who had passed their draft exams, and urged them to resist conscription into the military. The leaflets also claimed that the war was a "capitalist" war and we shouldn't be involved in it. He faced 20 years in prison. Schenck appealed on the basis that the First Amendment interposes a defense to the statute, thus, if the defense is valid the statute is invalid.

In upholding the conviction, the Court reasoned that, although the written content of the leaflets may ordinarily have been protected speech, the character of every act depends upon the circumstances under which it was done. Under the circumstances at that time, the Court held that restraint was necessary to prevent grave and immediate threats to national security—i.e., obstruction of the draft—and Congress had the right to prevent these threats. As Justice Holmes analogized: "The most stringent protection of free speech would not protect a man in falsely shouting fire in a theater and causing a panic."

In *Schenk*, Justice Holmes set forth a test: Whether the words employed are used in such circumstances and are of such a nature as to create a *clear and present danger* that they will bring about the substantive evil that Congress has a right to prevent. This was a "proximity and degree" analysis. Nevertheless, the majority did not agree with Holmes's clear and present danger formulation, although they agreed with the result, holding it to be a "bad tendency" test instead.

Frohwerk v. United States

One week following the *Schenk* decision, the Court again unanimously affirmed convictions under the Espionage Act in *Frohwerk v. United States*, 249 U.S., 204 (1919), stating:

"[W]e think it necessary to add to what has been said in Schenck v. United States . . . only that the First Amendment while prohibiting legislation against free speech as such cannot have been, and obviously was not, intended to give immunity for every possible use of language. We venture to believe that neither Hamilton nor Madison, nor any other competent person then or later, ever supposed that to make criminal the counseling of a murder within the jurisdiction of Congress would be an unconstitutional interference with free speech."

Abrams v. United States

A few months later, in *Abrams v. United States*, 250 U.S. 616 (1919), the Court upheld the conviction of another individual under the Espionage Act for distributing anti-war leaflets. Mr. Abrams protested military involvement in Russian foreign affairs. The majority again deferred to Congress as they had in *Schenck* and *Frohwerk*, holding that the First Amendment protections may be circumscribed by war.

However, Justice Holmes appeared to move away from his earlier holdings by enunciating a "case by case" analysis and a "clear and present danger" factor. In their dissent, Justice Holmes and Justice Brandeis rejected the application of *Schenck* and *Frohwerk*, and argued that speech could *only* be punished if it presented "a clear and present danger" of imminent harm, and that the Government had made no such showing.

The two Justices opined that mere political advocacy was protected by the First Amendment, and that they would have reversed the conviction because Abrams and his leaflets were not a likely hindrance to the war effort in Germany. As further set forth below, these Justices were eventually able to persuade a majority of the Court to adopt the "clear and present danger test," and the right to freedom of expression grew more secure for a period of time.

Gitlow v. New York

In *Gitlow v. New York*, 268 U.S. 652 (1925), the Court abandoned the "Holmes test" set forth in *Schenk*, when it affirmed the conviction of Gitlow—a member of the Socialist Party—for distributing a manifesto in violation of a law making it criminal to advocate, advise, or teach the duty, necessity, or propriety of overthrowing organized government by force or violence. There was no evidence regarding the effect of the distribution and no contention that it created any immediate threat to the security of the State. Nevertheless, the majority upheld the conviction using a "bad tendency" analysis.

Thus, the Court accepted a state legislative determination that statements advocating the overthrow of organized government by force, violence, and unlawful means, are so contrary to the general welfare, and involve such danger of substantive evil that they may be punished.

Justices Holmes and Brandeis again dissented, stating that *Gitlow* required a classic "clear and present danger" analysis. The Justices opined that if this analysis were undertaken, it would be obvious that the defendant's actions posed no real danger.

Whitney v. California

In a subsequent case, *Whitney v. California*, 274 U.S. 357 (1927), the majority accepted the state's determination of "danger to the public peace and security of the state," when it upheld the defendant's conviction under the California Criminal Syndicalism Act based upon her association with and membership in an organization which advocated the commission of criminal acts. It was charged that Mrs. Whitney assisted in the organization of the Communist Labor Party of California. Mrs. Whitney defended that she was organizing for political reform through the democratic process. However, since a majority at the convention advocated change through violence, she was convicted based on her presence at the convention, although she maintained that she had no knowledge of their illegal purpose.

The California state statute defined criminal syndicalism as any doctrine "advocating, teaching or aiding and abetting . . . crime . . . sabotage . . . or unlawful acts of force and violence to effect political or economic change. The tactic was to combat subversion by cutting off the "tentacles"—i.e., the members.

Conviction under a criminal syndicalism statute, unlike criminal conspiracy, did not require an overt act in furtherance of the conspiracy. For a conviction under criminal syndicalism, the government need only show that the individual joined the group knowingly because the crime *is* the fact of membership.

The Court stated that the fundamental right to free expression is not absolute and is subject to some restrictions, such as those required to protect the state from destruction or from "serious injury, political, economic or moral." Therefore, the Court held that it was necessary to devise a standard to determine (i) the degree of danger that justifiably requires protection by limiting expression; and (ii) how clear, imminent and likely that danger may be.

In general, this standard has been applied to utterances or writings which may incite, urge, counsel, advocate, or importune the commission of criminal conduct. The Supreme Court has also ruled that if the conduct is criminal, the advocacy or promotion of that conduct is also criminal.

Justice Brandeis again restated his view of the "clear and present danger" test in his dissent:

"[E]ven advocacy of violation [of the law] . . . is not a justification for denying free speech where the advocacy falls short of incitement and there is nothing to indicate that the advocacy would be immediately acted on. In order to support a finding of clear and present danger it must be shown either that immediate serious violence was to be expected or was advocated, or that the past conduct furnished reason to believe that such advocacy was then contemplated."

In the cases that followed *Whitney*, the Court did not summarily affirm convictions based on assertions made by the government.

Fiske v. Kansas

In *Fiske v. Kansas*, 274 U.S. 380 (1927), the Court held that a criminal syndicalism law had been invalidly applied to convict an individual where the only evidence was the "class struggle" language of the constitution of the organization to which he belonged.

Stromberg v. California

In *Stromberg v. California*, 283 U.S. 359 (1931), a conviction for violating a "red flag" law was voided as the statute was found unconstitutionally vague. It is notable that neither of the foregoing cases mentioned "clear and present danger."

Herndon v. Lowry

In *Herndon v. Lowry*, 301 U.S. 242, 258 (1937), the defendant was an organizer for the Communist Party. He had a box of membership blanks which stated that the aims of the party were to (i) advocate unemployment insurance; and (ii) promote equal rights for Blacks. He also had a booklet which advocated strikes and boycotts, and urged Southern states to be ruled by Blacks. He was convicted under the *Slave Insurrection Statute*, which had survived the Civil War because of its facial neutrality.

In a 5-4 decision overturning the conviction, the Court narrowly rejected the contention that the standard of guilt could be the "dangerous tendency" of one's words, because Herndon couldn't conceivably carry out the plans, and the State could not restrict words which only had a "tendency" to be dangerous. The Court held that the power of a State to prevent speech "must find its justification in a reasonable apprehension of danger to organized government," thus finally relying on Holmes' "clear and present danger" test.

Terminiello v. City of Chicago

In *Terminiello v. City of Chicago*, 337 U.S. 1 (1949), the defendant was convicted of disorderly conduct for using speech which caused a public riot. Applying the "clear and present danger" standard, in a 5-4 split decision, the Court overturned a conviction obtained after the trial judge instructed the jury that a breach of the peace could be committed by speech that "stirs the public to anger, invites dispute, brings about a condition of unrest, or creates a disturbance."

The Court held that the reactors, not the speaker, created the problem—i.e., the riot—and in the "marketplace of ideas," the government can't prevent speaking unless there is an imminent danger with what is said by the speaker.

For the majority, Justice Douglas opined:

"A function of free speech under our system of government is to invite dispute. It may indeed best serve its high purpose when it induces a condition of unrest, creates dissatisfaction with conditions as they are, or even stirs people to anger. Speech is often provocative and challenging. It may strike at prejudices and preconceptions and have profound unsettling effects as it presses for acceptance of an idea. That is why freedom of speech, though not absolute . . . is nevertheless protected against censorship or punishment, unless shown likely to produce a *clear and present danger* of a serious substantive evil that rises far above public inconvenience, annoyance, or unrest."

The dissent pointed out that rioting—a substantive evil—had already occurred as a result of the defendant's speech, and stated that the State has the right and the duty to prevent and punish. The dissent also opined that the evidence proved that danger of rioting and violence in response to the speech was "clear, present and immediate."

Feiner v. New York

The dissent's position in *Terminiello* was subsequently adopted in *Feiner v. New York*, 340 U.S. 315 (1951), wherein the Court upheld the conviction of the defendant under a state disorderly conduct statute. The defendant's speech included calling the President a "bum" and the American legion a "nazi gestapo." He urged Blacks to rise up in arms and fight for equal rights, and verbally attacked cops standing across the street. The audience reacted to his speech and threatened violence. Although police asked Feiner to stop, his friend refused on his behalf.

The majority deferred to the state and held that the arrest was not an attempt to censor the content of the speech, but an effort to protect the peace before the threatened violence took place. Chief Justice Vinson stated:

"[T]he findings of the state court as to the existing situation and the imminence of greater disorder coupled with petitioner's deliberate defiance of the police officers convince us that we should not reverse this conviction in the name of free speech."

Justices Douglas and Black vigorously dissented, pointing out that a minimal threat of violence was insufficient to suppress speech.

The Smith Act

In 1940, the Smith Act [Ch. 439, 54 Stat. 670 (1940) 18 U.S.C. Sec. 2385] was enacted which made it a criminal offense for anyone to knowingly or willfully advocate, abet, advise, or teach the duty, necessity, desirability, or propriety of overthrowing the government of the United States or of any State by force or violence, or for anyone to organize any association which teaches, advises, or encourages such an overthrow, or for anyone to become a member of, or to affiliate with, any such association.

It was not until 1951 that the Supreme Court finally stepped in to determine the degree to which the government was permitted to prosecute individuals and groups which it believed were conspiring to advocate and carry out the overthrow of the government pursuant to The Smith Act.

Dennis v. United States

In 1951, the Supreme Court, for the first time, reviewed a case prosecuted under The Smith Act. The case—*Dennis v. United States*, 341 U.S. 494 (1951)—involved the arrest of individuals for distribution of subversive Communist literature. In *Dennis*, the Supreme Court upheld convictions obtained under the Smith Act. In reaching its decision, the Court expounded upon the "clear and present danger" standard.

The defendants were arrested for distribution of subversive literature which spread the doctrine of a communist revolution by force. On appeal, they claimed that the Smith Act was unconstitutional, and violated the 1st, 5th and 14th Amendments. Justice Frankfurter, espousing a Blackstonian view, discussed the history leading up to adoption of the First Amendment, stating that the Bill of Rights was intended to set forth the guaranties and immunities inherited from English ancestry, *including* the well-recognized exceptions. Frankfurter further opined that the First Amendment was never intended to give unqualified immunity to every expression concerning matters of political interest.

The Court, while at the same time validating the "clear and present danger" standard, stated that the circumstances of each case should be considered instead of merely applying a rigid and inflexible rule. The Court adopted the lower court's interpretation of the rule, quoting Chief Judge Learned Hand:

> "In each case, the Court must ask whether the gravity of the evil, discounted by its improbability, justifies such invasion of free speech as is necessary to avoid the danger."

The *Dennis* case marked the beginning of the end of the "clear and present danger" test, and gave way to a "balancing test," as set forth by Justice Frankfurter in a concurring opinion:

> "The demands of free speech in a democratic society as well as the interest in national security are better served by candid and informed weighing of the competing interests, within the confines of the judicial process."

The Court concluded that the evil sought to be prevented was serious enough to justify suppression of speech, and stated that if the government is aware that a group advocating its overthrow is attempting to indoctrinate members and commit them to a course whereby they will strike when the leaders feel the circumstances permit, action by the government is required.

Thus, the "clear and present danger" standard virtually disappeared from Supreme Court decisions over the next 20 years, giving way to a "balancing" test, which is further discussed below.

Yates v. United States

In *Yates v. United States*, 354 U.S. 298 (1957), the Supreme Court set aside the convictions of several Communist Party leaders under the Smith Act, while at the same time acquitting some and remanding others for retrial. The decision was based on the faulty instructions the trial judge gave the jury. The trial judge advised the jury that all advocacy and teaching of forcible overthrow was punishable, whether it was language of incitement or not, provided it was done with an intent to accomplish that purpose.

The Supreme Court held, however, that the statute prohibited "advocacy of action," not merely "advocacy in the realm of ideas." The distinction between the two is that those to whom the advocacy is expressed must be urged to do something, now or in the future, rather than merely believe in something.

In addition, the Court found the general evidence submitted by the government concerning the Communist Party was insufficient to establish that the Communist Party had engaged in the required advocacy of action.

Membership as a Basis for Prosecution

It was a crime under The Smith Act to organize or become a member of an organization which teaches, advocates, or encourages the overthrow of government by force or violence. The consequences of being a member of an illegal organization could be severe. Aliens are subject to deportation for such membership, and the Court has sustained a statute requiring the termination of Social Security old age benefits to an alien who was deported on grounds of membership in the Communist Party.

Scales v. United States

In *Scales v. United States*, 367 U.S. 203 (1961), the Supreme Court affirmed the defendant's conviction under the Smith Act and held that it was constitutional under the First Amendment. Because the type of advocacy promoted by the Communist Party had been ruled unprotected under *Dennis*, the Court held that there was no reason why active membership in such a group, which is a purposeful form of complicity in the advocacy, should be protected.

Noto v. United States

In *Noto v. United States*, 367 U.S. 290 (1961), the Court reversed a conviction under the membership clause of the Smith Act because the evidence was insufficient to prove that the Communist Party had engaged in unlawful advocacy. The Court held that the mere abstract teaching of Communist theory is not the same as preparing a group for violent action and steering it to such action. There must be some substantial direct or circumstantial evidence of a call to violence, now or in the future.

Because of the Smith Act, the Government was also able to prosecute a number of Communist Party members based on their membership alone.

The Balancing of Interests Test

The "balancing test" used in *Dennis* first appeared in *American Communications Association v. Douds*, which was decided one year prior to the *Dennis* decision.

American Communications Association v. Douds

In *American Communications*, 339 U.S. 382 (1950), the Supreme Court sustained a law which required labor unions and their officers to sign an annual oath stating that they did not advocate the violent overthrow of the government and were not members of the Communist party. Those who did not sign the oath were barred from access to the National Labor Relations Board (NLRB).

In rejecting the "clear and present danger" test, the Court favored a balancing of interests test. According to Justice Vinson:

> "When particular conduct is regulated in the interest of public order, and the regulation results in an indirect, conditional, partial abridgement of speech, the duty of the courts is to determine which of these two conflicting interests demands the greater protection under the particular circumstances presented."

Thus, the Court viewed the government's right to prevent strikes and a disruption of commerce as more important than the limited interest of those alleging that their freedom of speech was being subverted. Nevertheless, the law was subsequently repealed.

During the 1950's and 1960's, the balancing test was used by the Court in deciding a number of cases involving the government's inquiries into, and attempts to regulate, the beliefs and associations of individuals. The government's position was that such beliefs and associations gave the government the ability to predict future or intended conduct that would be within the government's power to regulate or prohibit.

Konigsberg v. State Bar of California

In *Konigsberg v. State Bar of California*, 366 U.S. 36 (1961), the leading case on "balancing," the Court upheld a state's refusal to certify Mr. Konigsberg for admission to the bar. As a prerequisite for admission, an applicant was required to prove to the Committee of Bar Examiners that he was of "good moral character."

Although Konigsberg stated that he did not believe in the violent overthrow of the government, and that he had never knowingly been a member of any organization which advocated such action, he would not answer any questions pertaining specifically to membership in the Communist Party.

The Supreme Court applied a balancing of interests test in finding for the state, asserting that the government's interest was to make sure that those admitted to the practice of law were committed to lawful change in society. Thus, the Court held that it was proper for the state to believe that one who possessed a belief in the use of illegal means to change that form of government, which belief was firm enough to be carried over into advocacy, did not meet the standard of fitness.

The Court further stated that Konigsberg's First Amendment interest was limited because there was "minimal effect upon free association occasioned by compulsory disclosure" under the circumstances.

In his dissent, Justice Black expressed the absolutist view—i.e., the conviction that the government has no right to abridge freedom of expression whatsoever.   Justice Black's dissent turned out to be his longest and most articulate expression of his position against the "balancing of interests" test.

According to Justice Black, if a particular government regulation deterred or abridged speech, that was sufficient reason enough for him to find that the state's action was unconstitutional. He did not subscribe to the "balancing of interests" test as is demonstrated by his following statement:

> "I believe that the First Amendment's unequivocal command that there shall be no abridgment of the rights of free speech and assembly

shows that the men who drafted our Bill of Rights did all the balancing that was to be done in this field."

NAACP v. Alabama ex rel. Flowers

In 1964, free expression once again received needed support by the Supreme Court. In *NAACP v. Alabama ex rel. Flowers*, 377 U.S. 288 (1964), the state attempted to investigate the National Association for the Advancement of Colored People (NAACP), and obtain its membership lists. In this case, the Court again applied a balancing test and determined that the First Amendment rights of speech and association outweighed the government's interest.

Brandenburg v. Ohio—The Return of the Clear and Present Danger Standard

In *Brandenburg v. Ohio*, 395 U.S. 444 (1969), the Supreme Court struck down the conviction of a Ku Klux Klan member under Ohio's criminal syndicalism statute. The statute prohibited anyone from advocating the necessity or propriety of criminal or terroristic means to achieve political change. The defendant had been arrested for advocating political reform through violence and for assembling with a group to teach criminal syndicalism.

In reversing the conviction, the Court overruled *Whitney* without explicitly referring to the "clear and present danger" standard. It also eliminated the open-ended use of the tests that had prevailed in the "bad tendency" and "balancing" decisions. The Court reformulated its prior rulings and held that advocacy of the use of force or violence is protected under the First Amendment as long as the advocacy does not *incite* people to *imminent violence.*

Under the *Brandenburg* test, the state must prove that: (i) the speaker subjectively intended incitement; (ii) in context, the words used were likely to produce imminent, lawless action; and (iii) the words used by the speaker objectively encouraged and urged incitement.

Thus, *Brandenburg* provided new protection for strong advocacy. The focus is on the inciting language, objective words and the need to show not only that the speech is directed to produce immediate, unthinking, lawless action, but that, in fact, the situation makes this purpose likely to be successful. Mere teaching of abstract doctrines are not likely to lead a group to violent action, thus, any statute must be narrowly drawn to distinguish between what is advocacy of a theory and what is advocacy of action. The *Brandenberg* standard prevails today.

The McCarthy Era

In post-World War II America, there was much fear and concern about the infiltration of Communism. As a result, the United States government was always seeking to extinguish the Communist Party. During the "cold war and iron curtain" era, the fear of communism took on enormous significance. It should be noted, however, that the Russians were not involved with the U.S. Communist Party.

A disruptive and troubling event in American history involved the activities of Senator Joseph R. McCarthy during this time period in the early 1950's. McCarthy claimed that Communist agents had penetrated the federal government. Thus, the FBI infiltrated the Communist Party, which had essentially gone underground because convictions against members were routinely upheld.

Under the climate of this period—the "McCarthy Era"—the Supreme Court deferred to the witchhunt mentality of the time, seriously weakening the "clear and present danger" test. Individuals were punished for advocating the overthrow of the government even if the danger of such an occurrence were both slight and remote.

As a result, many individuals were prosecuted and jailed simply for advocating Communist revolution, and thousands lost their careers and their livelihood on the basis of unsubstantiated evidence. In fact, history professors so feared persecution that they changed their readings and chose not to present material which provided "two sides" of history. In 1954, the Senate condemned McCarthy and his political influence declined thereafter.

The Internal Security Act of 1950

Under The Internal Security Act of 1950, a comprehensive regulatory scheme was devised which would curb Communist-action organizations and Communist-front organizations. Under the Act, organizations found to fall within one or the other of these designations were required to (i) register with the Government; (ii) provide their membership lists for public inspection; (iii) provide accountings of all money received and expended; and (iv) provide lists of all printing presses and duplicating machines.

Members of organizations which failed to register were required to to do so or face criminal sanctions. A challenge under the Act reached the Supreme Court, which sustained the constitutionality of the Act under the First Amendment. Applying the balancing test, Justice Frankfurter, on behalf of the majority, concluded that the threat to national security posed by the Communist conspiracy outweighed considerations of individual liberty.

Those sections of the Act which required registration of Communist-action and Communist-front organizations and their members were subsequently repealed in 1968.

Suppression of Communist Propaganda in the Mail

In *Lamont v. Postmaster General*, 381 U.S. 301 (1965), the Supreme Court struck down a 1962 statute—Pub. L. 87-793, Sec. 305, 76 Stat. 840—which authorized the Post Office to retain all foreign mail determined to be "communist political propaganda" unless the recipient specifically requested the mail.

The Court held that the physical detention of mail upon the requirement that someone request that which has been designated by the government as undesirable violated the First Amendment right to receive information. This was the first federal law ever struck down by the Court as an infringement of the First Amendment speech and press clauses.

CHAPTER 5:

GOVERNMENT EMPLOYMENT AND RESTRICTIONS ON EXPRESSION

In General

As an employer, the Federal government has an obligation to ensure a harmonious workplace. As further set forth below, to achieve this end, some restriction on expression is inevitable. Nevertheless, any regulation which exceeds its purpose by unnecessarily infringing upon First Amendment rights will not be upheld.

Political Action Among Employees

In 1876, federal employees were prohibited from giving to, receiving or requesting money from another federal employee for political purposes. Shortly thereafter, the Civil Service Act of 1883 more broadly prohibited civil service employees from using their official authority or influence to coerce political action of any person or to interfere with elections. This goal was furthered by the Congressional enactment of the Hatch Act in 1939.

The Hatch Act

Under the Hatch Act—Ch. 410, 53 Stat. 1148 Sec. 9(a), (1939), as amended, 5 U.S.C. Sec. 7324(a)(2)—federal employees are forbidden to "take any active part in political management or in political campaigns."

The Act was extended to state and local government employees working in programs financed in whole or in part with federal funds, by a Congressional amendment—Ch. 640, 54 Stat. 767 (1940), as amended, 5 U.S.C. Sec. Sec. 1501-08. In *Oklahoma v. Civil Service Commission*, 330 U.S. 127 (1947), this provision withstood a federalism challenge. All the States have since adopted laws patterned on the Hatch Act.

The Hatch Act prevents employees from running for public office, distributing campaign literature, playing an active role at political meetings, circulating nomination petitions, attending political conventions, except as spectators, publishing letters soliciting votes for candidates, and all similar activities.

United Public Workers v. Mitchell

In *United Public Workers v. Mitchell*, 330 U.S. 75, 94-104 (1947), the question arose as to whether government, which may not prohibit citizens in general from engaging in these activities, may still regulate such activities by its own employees when they are off-duty. The Supreme Court ruled that it could.

Although the Court recognized that the restriction of political activities imposed by the Act did in some measure impair First Amendment rights, it reiterated the established principle that no right is absolute. The Court emphasized that the substantial Government interest in forbidding partisan political activities by its employees overrode their right to engage in political activities and association.

Loyalty Oaths

Significant First Amendment issues are often raised concerning loyalty standards for government employees. The government may establish a system to investigate employees pursuant to loyalty standards, or it may require employees to subscribe to a loyalty oath which disclaims belief in, advocacy of, or membership in an organization which advocates illegal or disloyal action.

Although the Supreme Court has not constitutionally confronted such initiatives as they apply to the Federal Government, the Court has encountered state loyalty oath programs. For example, in *Gerende v. Board of Supervisors of Elections*, 341 U.S. 56 (1951), the Court upheld a state court construction requiring candidates for public office to make an oath that he or she is not engaged in "the attempt to overthrow the government by force or violence . . . and not knowingly a member of an organization engaged in such an attempt."

The Court also upheld a state requirement that employees make a loyalty oath that they had not "advised, advocated, or taught the overthrow of government by unlawful means, nor been a member of an organization with similar objectives." In addition, the employees were also required to swear that they were not and had never been members of the Communist Party.

The Court held that the oath requirement was valid as "a reasonable regulation to protect the municipal service by establishing an employment qualification of loyalty" and as being "reasonably designed to protect the integrity and competency of the service."

The Court has also held that a state could deny employment based on a person's advocacy of overthrow of the government by force or violence, or based on unexplained membership in an organization which so advocates, with knowledge of the advocacy. However, the Court did strike down a state oath requirement disqualifying employees and prospective employees from employment "solely on the basis of organizational membership." The Court held that the employee must have knowledge of the organization's illegal aims.

For example, in *Keyishian v. Board of Regents*, 385 U.S. 589, 597-604 (1967), the Court held that "legislation which sanctions membership unaccompanied by specific intent to further the unlawful goals of the organization or which is not active membership violates constitutional limitations." Nevertheless, subsequent cases firmly reiterated the power of governmental agencies to inquire into the associational relationships of their employees, and has upheld statutes which are narrowly drawn.

CHAPTER 6:

SYMBOLIC SPEECH AND EXPRESSIVE CONDUCT

In General

The communication of ideas is not carried out merely through the exchange of words or publication, but often involves what is known as "symbolic speech" or "expressive conduct." For the purposes of this almanac, the term "symbolic speech" will be used to describe any type of nonverbal expression used to communicate a political, economic, social or other viewpoint.

Symbolic speech is generally protected under the First Amendment, and may include music lyrics; slogans on t-shirts; wearing symbols, such as political buttons and armbands; picketing; distributing literature; and participating in demonstrations and marches.

Nevertheless, because symbolic speech generally involves action and not simply words, it is subject to more regulation and restriction than mere speech. The First Amendment is concerned with the degree to which these actions are intended to communicate a point of view so as to trigger the right of free expression. As further discussed herein, certain types of symbolic speech have resulted in controversy and an attempt at restricting free speech rights through legislative efforts.

Public Forum

In general, case law has held that public streets and parks, including those adjacent to courthouses and foreign embassies, as well as public libraries and the grounds of legislative bodies, are open to public demonstrations. Nevertheless, The First Amendment does not guarantee access to property simply because it is owned or controlled by the government.

For example, the use to which the public area is dedicated may impinge on the type of protected expression sought to be conducted there. The Supreme Court has held that the crucial question is whether the manner of expression is basically compatible with the normal activity of a particular place at a particular time. However, if the government does open non-traditional arenas for expressive activities, it may not discriminate on the basis of content or viewpoint in granting access to any particular group.

Private Property

Determining whether private property may be used as a "public forum" has created some difficulty for the Court. In some instances, the Court has held that private property is so functionally similar to public property that private owners may not forbid symbolic speech being conducted on the property.

For example, in *Marsh v. Alabama*, 326 U.S. 501 (1946), the Court held that the private owner of a company-owned town could not forbid the distribution of religious materials by a Jehovah's Witness on a downtown street. In reaching its decision, the Court found that the town had all the attributes of any American municipality, and functioned like any other town, although it was wholly owned by the corporation. The Court reasoned:

"[T]he more an owner, for his advantage, opens up his property for use by the public in general, the more do his rights become circumscribed by the statutory and constitutional rights of those who use it."

On the other hand, in *Lloyd Corp. v. Tanner*, 407 U.S. 551 (1972), the Court upheld a state trespass law which banned anti-war protesters from distributing leaflets in the mall of a shopping center. The Court held that the shopping center had not dedicated its property to a public use but had only invited the public for the specific purpose of doing business with the stores located in the center.

In a subsequent case, *Hudgens v. NLRB*, 424 U.S. 507 (1976), the Court specifically ruled that shopping centers are not functionally equivalent to the company town in *Marsh*.

Time/Place/Manner Restrictions

As set forth in Chapter 2, speech in public places is subject to time, place, and manner restrictions. Nevertheless, these regulations are closely scrutinized and, to be upheld, must be content-neutral; serve a significant governmental interest; and provide for substantial alternative opportunities for expression.

Picketing

The Supreme Court has held that picketing by a labor union is entitled to First Amendment protection. In *Thornhill v. Alabama*, 310 U.S. 88 (1940), the Court struck down a ban on picketing, stating:

"In the circumstances of our times the dissemination of information concerning the facts of a labor dispute must be regarded as within that area of free discussion that is guaranteed by the Constitution."

Nevertheless, in *Milk Wagon Drivers Union v. Meadowmoor Dairies*, 312 U.S. 287 (1941), the Court did proscribe peaceful picketing under circumstances in which violence had already occurred and was likely to continue.

Ultimately, in *International Brotherhood of Teamsters v. Vogt, 354 U.S. 284, 293 (1957)*, the Court, in deference to state public policy, recognized the necessity of placing some restrictions on picketing:

"[A] state, in enforcing some public policy, whether of its criminal or its civil law, and whether announced by its legislature or its courts, could constitutionally enjoin peaceful picketing aimed at preventing effectuation of that policy."

Demonstrations and Parades

The Supreme Court has generally refused to permit restrictions on demonstrations and parades, and has reversed convictions obtained for offenses such as breach of the peace, when the Court believed the disturbance had resulted from opposition to the demonstrator's protected speech.

NAACP v. Claiborne Hardware Co.

In a landmark case, *NAACP v. Claiborne Hardware Co.*, 458 U.S. 886 (1982), a unanimous Court held that the states must observe new and enhanced constitutional standards in order to impose liability upon persons for engaging in expressive conduct implicating the First Amendment.

In that case, black citizens of a Mississippi town organized to protest racial conditions in the town. They sought desegregation of public facilities, hiring of black policemen, hiring of more black employees by local stores, and the end to verbal abuse by police. The group decided to boycott the town's white merchants, and to deliver speeches to convince others to boycott the establishments.

In response, the Mississippi Supreme Court imposed joint and several liability upon leaders and participants of the boycott, and upon the NAACP, for lost earnings suffered by the merchants. The lawsuit was based on the common law tort of malicious interference with business. The Court further held that because there were sporadic acts of violence associated with the boycott, it lost any First Amendment protection to which it may have been entitled.

The Supreme Court reversed the lower court, holding that the boycott was legal and, for the most part, was constitutionally protected. The Court further held that violence alone did not deprive the other activities of First Amendment protection. In that connection the Court stated:

"The First Amendment does not protect violence . . . No federal rule of law restricts a State from imposing tort liability for business losses that are caused by violence and by threats of violence. When such conduct occurs in the context of constitutionally protected activity, however, precision of regulation is demanded . . . Specifically, the presence of activity protected by the First Amendment imposes restraints on the grounds that may give rise to damages liability and on the persons who may be held accountable for those damages."

Thus, although states may impose damages for the consequences of violent conduct, they may not award compensation for the consequences of nonviolent, protected activity.

In this case, the state was permitted to compensate any merchants who could prove the measure of their damages that resulted from violence as opposed to the losses suffered as a result of the protected boycott and accompanying speeches. Further, the only individuals liable for such damages were those who actually committed the violent acts, and those nonviolent individuals who associated with them, aware of the violence and possessing an intent to further it.

Leafleting

The Supreme Court has held that the distribution of pamphlets and leaflets is constitutionally protected under the First Amendment and has historically been a powerful weapon in defense of liberty. State courts have attempted to ban leafleting under littering prohibitions, however, such attempts have been struck down as insufficient to justify infringing upon the exercise of free speech rights.

In *Schneider v. Town of Irvington*, 308 U.S. 147, 161, 162 (1939), the Court struck down one such statute, stating:

"We are of the opinion that the purpose to keep the streets clean and of good appearance is insufficient to justify an ordinance which prohibits a person rightfully on a public street from handing literature to one willing to receive it. Any burden imposed upon the city

authorities in cleaning and caring for the streets as an indirect consequence of such distribution results from the constitutional protection
of the freedom of speech and press."

Door-to-Door Solicitation

In *Martin v. City of Struthers*, 319 U.S. 141, 147 (1943), the Court struck
down an ordinance which sought to ban door-to-door solicitation on privacy
and safety grounds. In balancing the respective interests, the Court held:

"[T]he dangers of distribution can so easily be controlled by tradi-
tional legal methods, leaving to each householder the full right to decide whether he will receive strangers as visitors, that stringent
prohibition can serve no purpose but that forbidden by the Constitution, the naked restriction of the dissemination of ideas."

Nevertheless, the Court subsequently noted that a municipality does have
the right to protect its citizens from crime and annoyance by regulating
door-to-door solicitation. However, in order to be valid, the ordinance must
be narrowly drawn and cannot give the municipality the right to make this
determination based on the content of the solicitation.

Flag Desecration

A popular type of "symbolic speech" conducted by demonstrators in the
1960's and 1970's, in large part as a result of anti-Vietnam War sentiment,
was burning or otherwise desecrating the American flag. This particular
type of expression has been a source of division for the Supreme Court, even
to this day.

In *Street v. New York*, 394 U.S. 576 (1969), the defendant was convicted
under a state statute punishing desecration "by words or act" upon evidence
that he burned the flag while speaking contemptuous words. The Court set
aside the conviction holding that there was no valid governmental interest
supported penalizing verbal contempt for the flag.

Nevertheless, Justices Warren, Black, White and Fortas issued a strong
dissent concluding that the First Amendment did not preclude a flat pro-
scription of flag burning or flag desecration for expressive purposes.

Most recently, in 1989 and again in 1990, a divided Court, in a 5-4 vote,
held that prosecutions for flag burning at a public demonstration violated the
First Amendment. In *Texas v. Johnson*, 491 U.S. 397 (1989), the Court rejected a state flag desecration statute designed to protect the flag's symbolic
value. Subsequently, in *United States v. Eichman*, 496 U.S. 310 (1990), the

Court rejected a more limited federal statute purporting to protect only the flag's physical integrity.

The Texas statute invalidated in *Johnson* defined the prohibited act as any physical mistreatment of the flag that the actor knew would seriously offend other persons. The Court held that placing an emphasis on causing offense to others meant that the law was not "unrelated to the suppression of free expression." The *Johnson* decision paved the way for the fate of the existing Federal statute subsequently struck down in *Eichman*, as well as state flag desecration statutes.

Proposed Legislation to Prohibit Flag Desecration

As a result of these Supreme Court decisions, there has been a concerted effort by both the House of Representatives and the Senate to pass legislation that will ban desecration of the American flag. The following proposed legislation is pending:

The Flag Protection Act of 1999

The Flag Protection Act of 1999, introduced in the House of Representatives on March 11, 1999, seeks to amend the Federal criminal code to revise provisions regarding desecration of the flag to set penalties with respect to persons who:

(1) destroy or damage a U.S. flag with intent to provoke, and in circumstances reasonably likely to produce, imminent violence or a breach of the peace;

(2) steal or knowingly convert to their use, or the use of another, a U.S. flag belonging to the United States and intentionally destroy or damage that flag; and

(3) within any lands reserved for the use of the United States, or under the exclusive or concurrent jurisdiction thereof, steal or knowingly convert to their use, or the use of another, a U.S. flag belonging to another person and intentionally destroy or damage that flag.

The Act also expresses the sense of the Congress that the States should enact prohibitions similar to the provisions of this Act.

The text of the Flag Protection Act of 1999 is set forth at Appendix 4.

Senate Judiciary Resolution 14: A Joint Resolution Proposing a Constitutional Amendment to Declare that Congress has the Power to Prohibit Physical Desecration of the Flag

Senate Judiciary Resolution 14 (S.J. Res. 14), introduced in the Senate on March 17, 1999, seeks to declare, by constitutional amendment, that Congress shall have the power to prohibit the physical desecration of the U.S. flag.

The text of S.J. Res. 14 is set forth at Appendix 5.

Opposition to Flag Protection Legislation

Opponents of the proposed flag protection legislation argue that, although flag burning can be deeply offensive, it is nonetheless political speech, and that such an amendment would infringe on the fundamental right to protest and criticize the government.

On March 25, 1999, Solange E. Bitol, Legislative Counsel for the American Civil Liberties Union (ACLU), submitted a statement before the U.S. Senate Judiciary Committee in opposition to the proposed flag desecration legislation. The text of the ACLU's opposition statement is set forth at Appendix 6.

Symbolic Conduct Interfering with the War Effort

The Supreme Court has determined that certain types of symbolic conduct aimed at undermining the war effort are not protected under the First Amendment. For example, the Vietnam War was a very unpopular war which eventually resulted in a purposeful and organized resistance to both the war and the military draft. There were a number of marches, sit-ins, and demonstrations opposing America's involvement in the war.

As set forth below, the Supreme Court upheld the conviction of an individual who participated in symbolic anti-war conduct on the basis of sufficient governmental interest, yet reversed the conviction of an individual arrested for employing certain other types of symbolic anti-war expressions.

United States v. O'Brien

In *United States v. O'Brien*, 391 U.S. 367 (1968), the Supreme Court affirmed a conviction under a congressional prohibition against destruction of draft cards in the face of a claim that the conviction violated the defendant's First Amendment right of expression.

The defendant was prosecuted for publicly burning his draft card during an anti-war demonstration. The Court held that the defendant's conduct was not a constitutionally protected activity, even though it was argued that the conduct constituted the expression of an idea which was protected under the First Amendment.

The Court held that when speech and nonspeech elements are combined in the same course of conduct, a sufficiently important governmental interest in regulating the nonspeech element can justify incidental limitations on First Amendment freedoms.

The Court recently upheld a passive enforcement policy which singles out for prosecution those who fail to register and notify the authorities of their intention not to register or for whom the government receives a report concerning their intention not to register.

Cohen v. California

In *Cohen v. California*, 403 U.S. 15 (1971), the Supreme Court reversed the conviction of a man who was arrested for wearing a t-shirt displaying an offensive four-letter expletive concerning the military draft. The Court recognized that people in public places must be subject to some objectionable speech.

Justice Harlan stated that the ability of government to constitutionally shut off discourse solely to protect others from hearing it is dependent upon a showing that substantial privacy interests are being invaded in an essentially intolerable manner. The fact that an offensive expletive was used does not detract from protection because "one man's vulgarity is another man's lyric." The offensive words were not a direct, personal insult specifically aimed at the listener.

Anti-Abortion Protests and RICO

Following the legalization of abortion in 1973, pro-life activists began peaceful picketing and demonstrating outside abortion clinics. However, a radical element of the anti-abortion movement turned what may have been protected peaceful protesting into a campaign of violence. They harassed and intimidated patients of the clinics, and blocked their entry. More recently, their violent actions have included clinic bombings, assaults, and even the murder of clinic doctors. In October 1998, Dr. Barnett Slepian was the seventh obstetrician to succumb to anti-abortion violence.

Under the First Amendment, those opposed to abortion have the right to demonstrate and picket outside of abortion clinics. However, they do not have the right to block the entry of the clinic. Thus, the Supreme Court has upheld injunctions prohibiting the protestors from demonstrating directly outside of two clinics which had been subjected to particularly intrusive conduct, including "physical obstruction, intimidation, harassment, crowding, grabbing, and screaming."

The Racketeer Influenced and Corrupt Organizations Law of 1970 (RICO)

Under the federal Racketeer Influenced and Corrupt Organizations Law of 1970 ("RICO"), individuals involved in a "criminal enterprise" are subject to prosecution and liable for treble damages in civil actions brought by victims. The statute was originally enacted to target organized crime.

In April 1998, the National Organization for Women ("NOW") obtained a favorable verdict in a class action lawsuit against radical anti-abortion organizations, using RICO as a basis for the action. The lawsuit basically claimed that the defendants were guilty of "extortion" in attempting to put abortion clinics out of business. If the verdict survives an appeal, it would greatly limit protesting by anti-abortion radicals.

Although violence against abortion clinics is certainly disfavored, those concerned with protecting First Amendment rights have criticized the use of RICO against political movements, claiming that it will have the effect of chilling political speech. RICO does not target individual acts of violence, but seeks to destroy the entire "criminal" enterprise. Because most anti-abortion protesting is legal and protected speech, they argue that the use of RICO would have the effect of restricting both protected and unprotected speech. They also fear that RICO will backfire and ultimately be used to curtail other types of politically motivated conduct.

CHAPTER 7:

OBSCENITY

Early History of Censorship

Under English law, the rule for judging obscenity as formulated by Justice Cockburn provided:

> "[T]he test of obscenity is whether the tendency of the matter charged as obscenity is to deprave and corrupt those whose minds are open to such immoral influences, and into whose hands a publication of this sort may fall."

This test became the guiding principle for the majority of English and American courts. Nevertheless, American standards of decency have changed so drastically over the centuries that the values and restrictions of the early Puritan era are now unimaginable.

It was not until the mid-19th century that a censorship movement began to block so-called "indecent literature." The movement was spearheaded by a Connecticut man named Anthony Comstock. Comstock was responsible for organizing the New York Society for Suppression of Vice which, under New York law, was empowered with the rights to search, seize and arrest. Under The Comstock Act of 1873, all material found to be "lewd," "indecent," "filthy," or "obscene," was banned. Following this lead, a number of other similar organizations sprung up across the country.

In addition, a federal law entitled the "Comstock Law," was passed which forbid sending obscene materials through the mail. A number of prosecutions were undertaken under this law. During the Comstock era, many books were banned and thousands of people were arrested. Books by such literary greats as Chaucer, Hemingway, Steinbeck, F. Scott Fitzgerald, and D.H. Lawrence, to name a few, were banned at one time or another under obscenity laws. However, during the 20th century, censorship began to fall into disfavor, and the judiciary was called upon to set a clear path.

In 1933, in a landmark federal case involving the book *Ulysses* by James Joyce, Judge John Woolsey opined that the book "must be tested by the Court's opinion as to its effect on a person with average sex instincts ... who plays . . . the same role . . . as does the *reasonable man in the law of torts.*"

In 1948, another landmark case involved the raid of over fifty Philadelphia bookstores and the seizure of two-thousand books alleged to be obscene. In formulating a decision, the presiding judge addressed the concern for protection of young children, when he stated:

> "It will be asked whether one would care to have one's young daughter read these books. I suppose that by the time she is old enough to wish to read them she will have learned the biologic facts of life and the words that go with them. . . Our daughters must live in the world and decide what sort of women they are to be, and we should be willing to prefer their deliberate and informed choice of decency rather than an innocence that continues to spring from ignorance."

In 1957, the Supreme Court invalidated a Michigan statute which purported to protect the youth by censoring certain books. The Court addressed the legislative purpose by stating:

> "The State of Michigan insists that, by thus quarantining the general reading public against books not too rugged for grown men and women in order to shield juvenile innocence, it is exercising its power to protect the general welfare. Surely this is to burn the house to roast the pig. The incidence of this enactment is to reduce the adult population of Michigan to reading only what is fit for children."

The Supreme Court has continued to strike down censorship as an affront against the First Amendment. According to Justice Douglas: "[I]f a board of censors can tell the American people what it is in their best interests to see or to read or to hear then . . . the great purpose of the First Amendment to keep uncontrolled the freedom of expression is defeated."

The Present-Day Obscenity Standard

In *Miller v. California*, 413 U.S. 15 (1973), the Supreme Court attempted to establish an obscenity standard consisting of three conditions. In order to be considered legally obscene, a work must:

    1. Appeal to the average person's prurient interest in sex;

    2. Depict sexual conduct in a patently offensive way as defined by community standards; and

    3. Taken as a whole, lack serious literary, artistic, political or scientific value.

Despite the Court's attempt to devise a test, defining obscenity is still a difficult task. In that regard, a statement by Justice Potter Stewart is often quoted: "I know it when I see it."

Protection of Minors

Sexual content has traditionally been at the core of censorship debates. However, the First Amendment has since extended somewhat of a blanket protection over sexual materials directed towards adults. Nevertheless, censorship disputes continue to arise when children are exposed to materials and information involving sex, and the concern is inevitably raised that such exposure is "harmful" to a child.

Five years before the *Miller* test was established, the Supreme Court formulated a different standard concerning access to sexual material by minors in *Ginsberg v. New York*, 390 U.S. 629 (1968). In *Ginsberg*, the Court upheld a New York statute which criminalized the distribution of material deemed "harmful to minors" without a showing of *actual harm* or a *compelling* state interest. The Court ruled:

> "[T]he concept of obscenity . . . may vary according to the group to whom the questionable material is directed . . . Because of the State's exigent interest in preventing distribution to children of objectionable material, it can exercise its power to protect the health, safety, welfare and morals of its community by barring the distribution to children of books recognized to be suitable for adults."

Thus, material that appeals to the "prurient, shameful or morbid" interest of minors; lacks serious social value for minors; and is "patently offensive" based on adult views of what is fit for minors, may be deemed "harmful to minors."

Subsequently, in *New York v. Ferber*, 73 L. Ed. 2D 1113 (1982), the Court also upheld restrictions on various *depictions* of minors that could be considered sexual, citing the compelling need to protect actual children from possible exploitation by child pornographers. The question remains unanswered, however, whether any such material that has literary, historical, scientific or artistic value would be protected.

In 1990, in *Osborne v. Ohio* 495 U.S. 103 (1990), the Court went even further in its endeavor to protect children, and upheld a law which criminalizes an adult's possession of child pornography in his own home.

The Child Pornography Protection Act of 1996

The Supreme Court routinely upholds laws protecting minors from sexual exploitation and child pornography. In 1996, Congress decided to strengthen those laws and included additional legislation—known as the Child Pornography Protection Act of 1996 ("CPPA")—in the Federal budget bill.   Prior to passage of the Act, illegal child pornography only involved depictions of actual children engaged in sexually explicit activity.

The CPPA criminalizes not only sexual images involving actual children, but also criminalizes the use of computer-generated images, the use of adult "body doubles," and sexual images that appear to be minors, or that are advertised as minors, even if no minors are actually involved. Violators of the law face mandatory prison sentences of 15 years.

Thus, the CPPA expands the definition of illegal child pornography to include images not necessarily based on real children. The theory behind the law is that such images encourage pedophilia. Opponents of the CPPA argue that the statute goes too far because it does not recognize materials that may have artistic, historical, scientific, literary or other value, as protected under the First Amendment. In addition, they argue, under the law as written, movie scenes in which an adult portrays a minor—under the age of 18—engaged in sexual activity would be outlawed.

Thus far, the CPPA has been unsuccessfully challenged in the relatively few courts who have been called on to consider its constitutionality. One federal district court found it unconstitutionally vague and overbroad, but that decision was reversed on appeal. Another court upheld the statute on the theory that such materials facilitate sexual exploitation of children. Most recently, an appeal has been filed in the federal appeals court of San Francisco in the case of *Free Speech Coalition v. Reno* challenging the constitutionality of the CPPA.

The text of the Child Pornography Protection Act of 1996 is set forth at Appendix 7.

CHAPTER 8:

ARTS AND ENTERTAINMENT

In General

Protection of the First Amendment right of freedom of expression in America has been fervently protected over the years. Nevertheless, the framers of the Constitution could not have imagined television, movies and the internet, and the type of provocative and controversial images and ideas that they exhibit.

Proponents of censorship argue that the murder, violence and explicit sexual images portrayed in the media should not be protected, as they often offend religious beliefs, degrade women, and endanger children. However, defenders of First Amendment rights argue that a free society is based on the principle that each and every individual has the right to decide the type of entertainment he or she wants to accept or reject, and that the government has no right to make that decision. They suggest that those who may be offended by violence or sexual images should merely refrain from watching a particular movie or television program, and concerned parents can prevent access to certain programming through the use of available blocking devices.

Artistic Freedom

Artistic freedom is protected under the First Amendment, and has been interpreted by the Supreme Court to include a broad spectrum of artistic expression, including books, paintings, music, sculptures, theater, movies, television, and magazines, etc. When the Supreme Court is called upon to determine whether there has been an infringement on artistic expression, they generally conduct a two-part analysis:

Content Neutral

There can be no censorship or restriction on artistic expression merely because the content offends the listener, even if that viewpoint is shared by the majority.

Direct and Imminent Harm

Artistic expression may be restricted if it will cause clear *direct and imminent* harm to an important societal interest.

Television Programming

Violent Content

Proponents of censorship argue that violent images on television may cause people, and children in particular, to act in more aggressive and destructive ways. If it could be proven that exposure to violence in the media resulted in violent actions in real life, there would be a compelling reason to censor such images.   Opponents argue that there is no evidence that fictional violence causes otherwise balanced people to become violent.

Scientific studies on the correlation between violence in the media and actual violence have been conducted and are subject to debate. Children who have been exposed to violent television programming have been shown to temporarily act more aggressively during play following this exposure. However, the problem with any study is the old "chicken and the egg" quandary—it is near impossible to determine whether individuals who are already prone to aggression are also drawn to violent programming, or whether the violent programming causes the aggressive behavior.

Sexual Content

Most censorship movements target sexual content in the television industry. Although the Supreme Court has allowed censorship of "sexual speech" on moral grounds, not all sexual expression can be suppressed. As more fully set forth in Chapter 7, only a narrow range of obscene materials are restricted.

Nevertheless, although the Supreme Court has held that indecent expression is entitled to some degree of constitutional protection, it has held that indecency in some media may be regulated:

Federal Communications Commission v. Pacifica Foundation

In *Federal Communications Commission v. Pacifica*, 438 U.S. 726 (1978), the Court ruled that the government could require radio and television stations to broadcast "indecent" material only during programming hours when children would be least likely to view or listen. The Court defined "broadcast indecency" as "language that describes, in terms patently offensive as measured by contemporary community standards for the broadcast medium, sexual or excretory activities or organs."

TV Parental Guidelines

In July 1997, the major networks, with the exception of NBC, agreed to begin using TV Parental Guidelines—a television rating system that designates S for sex, V for violence, L for foul language, D for suggestive dialogue and FV for fantasy violence. News and sports programming are exempt from the rating system.

The TV parental guidelines were introduced to supplement the television rating system that was modeled after the movie rating system: TV-G (general audiences), TV-PG (parental guidance suggested), TV-Y7 and TV-14 (programs unsuitable for children under 7 and 14, respectively) and TV-MA (mature audiences only).

Proponents of the rating system believe that it will have a positive affect on the content of television programming because programs that receive unfavorable ratings may be abandoned by advertisers.

The Violence Chip

Both the Senate and the House of Representatives have devised legislation which requires new televisions to be equipped with a violence chip—known as the "v-chip"—which is a computer chip capable of detecting and blocking adversely rated programming. Under the Senate version of the bill, the television industry is required to establish a rating system for violence and other objectionable content or the Senate will authorize the appointment of a federal ratings agency.

Under the House version of the bill, a government advisory committee would be established to set guidelines for rating programs that contain sexual, violent, or other indecent material. The respective bills are being considered in committee to resolve any differences before they are finally passed.

Opponents of the v-chip argue that, instead of giving parents control over their children's viewing, it actually usurps parental control in that it is the government—not the parents—who will determine how programming will be rated once the chip is activated.

Popular Music

Parents' groups and religious fundamentalists have organized to challenge the content of popular music since the 1980's. For example, the Parents' Music Resource Center (PMRC) has called for the labeling of recordings which include topics related to drugs and alcohol, suicide, violence or sex. Record companies, artists and storeowners have also been subject to prosecution for producing or selling albums that contain controversial songs.

For example, in the late 1980s, state prosecutors brought a criminal obscenity charge against the owner of a record store for selling an album by the rap group known as *2 Live Crew* called "As Nasty As They Wanna Be." This was the first time that obscenity charges had ever been brought against song lyrics. Nevertheless, on appeal, the U.S. Court of Appeals for the Eleventh Circuit held that the record could not be regarded as obscene. *Luke Records, Inc. v. Navarro*, 960 F.2d 134, 135 (11th Cir.), cert. denied, 113 S. Ct. 659 (1992). The Court ruled: "[B]ecause music possesses inherent artistic value, no work of music alone may be declared obscene."

In addition, Singer Ozzy Osbourne was sued three times by parents who claimed that their sons killed themselves as a result of listening to his song entitled "Suicide Solution."

Labeling System

Following a series of Senate hearings conducted in 1985, and pressure from groups such as the PMRC, in 1990, the Recording Industry Association of America (RIAA) introduced a uniform labeling system. Under the RIAA system, the record companies decide which music is so controversial that it requires a label stating: "Parental Advisory—Explicit Lyrics." In practice, the only music being subjected to the labeling criteria is rap music and rock music.

Nevertheless, there is a call for even greater restrictions on the sale of music with controversial lyrics. Many states are considering legislation that would require more detailed warnings labels than that proposed by the RIAA, and a ban on the sale of particularly offensive music to minors. For example, a bill proposed by New Jersey would require a parental advisory label on music lyrics that discuss suicide; incest; bestiality; sadomasochism; rape or involuntary sexual penetration; or which advocate or encourage murder; ethnic, racial or religious intimidation; the use of illegal drugs; or the excessive or illegal use of alcohol.

Opponents of the labeling system argue that such restrictions are arbitrary and vague, making it impossible for artists, record companies and stores to understand whether or how the laws apply to them. They fear this could lead to self-censorship to avoid any possibility of criminal prosecution. The correct remedy, they argue, is that those who object to certain music lyrics use their own free-speech rights—e.g. pickets and boycotts—to bring their view to the public that such lyrics are harmful.

Regulating the Internet

There is much concern over the type of material available to children over the internet. In fact, in large part due to stories about child solicitation occurring over the internet, and the ready availability of on-line pornography, there is more recent distress over internet content than the violence and sex in television programming.

The Communications Decency Act of 1996

The Communications Decency Act (CDA), made it a crime to transmit indecent speech to minors on-line. However, the CDA was declared unconstitutional by the United States Supreme Court in *ACLU v. Reno*, 929 F. Supp. 824 (1996). According to the Court, the CDA imposed an unconstitutional censorship scheme on the internet, described by a federal judge as "the most participatory form of mass speech yet developed." The ruling basically gave the internet the same protection accorded books and other printed materials.

The Child Online Protection Act of 1998

In response to the *Reno* ruling, Congress enacted the Child Online Protection Act in October 1998. The Act has been dubbed "CDA II"—as successor to the invalidated CDA.

President Clinton signed the bill, notwithstanding the fact that the United States Department of Justice expressed reservations about its constitutionality. Almost immediately following its passage, the Act was challenged on the ground that it violates the First Amendment, as applied by the Supreme Court in *Reno*.

Title I: Protection from Material that is Harmful to Minors

Under Title I of the Act, material deemed "harmful to minors" on commercial internet sites is prohibited. Minors are defined as children under the age of 17. An affirmative defense under the Act is the website: (1) requires the use of a credit card, debit account, adult access code, or adult personal identification number; (2) accepts a digital certificate that verifies age; or (3) uses other reasonable age verification measures.

Title II: Children's Online Privacy Protection

Under Title II, it is unlawful for an operator of a website or online service directed towards children under the age of 13, or any operator that has actual knowledge that it is collecting personal information from a child, to collect personal information from such child in a manner that violates the Act.

The text of the Child Online Protection Act is set forth at Appendix 8.

Filtering

As a result of the *Reno* decision, a number of proposals have been suggested to restrict the availability of controversial content to minors over the internet, and the White House has requested voluntary cooperation in rating and blocking offensive on-line speech.

Filtering Software

Filtering software which blocks access to certain websites, and/or edits out offensive on-line speech, is marketed to individual users as well as schools and libraries. Opponents to the filtering system, such as the American Library Association (ALA), argue that filters block an extensive amount of useful information because they are unable to discriminate based on context. Therefore, important information concerning, e.g., sex education and health matters, would be filtered out regardless of its worth. In addition, because blocking is carried out by the software vendor, filtering takes away individual choice, imposes filtering on everyone, and treats users of all ages identically, without allowing the consumer to determine what and why certain information may be unavailable.

Platform for Internet Content Selection (PICS)

Unlike filtering software, PICS is a protocol for exchanging rating information by which the user chooses a rating system and then installs software to filter content. It is also embedded in the Web browsers of certain systems, such as Microsoft. The browser is able to read v-chip type ratings from software, or website publishers.

The Safe Schools Internet Act of 1999 (H.R. 368)

Legislation was introduced in the House of Representatives on January 19, 1999 by Representative Bob Franks to try to address the problem of inappropriate matter available to minors on the internet. The Act seeks to amend the Communications Act of 1934 to prohibit universal telecommunications services from being provided to any elementary or secondary school unless its administrator has certified to the Federal Communications Commission (FCC) that it has selected and installed a system for computers with internet access which filters or blocks matters deemed inappropriate for minors.

The Act prohibits internet access to a library unless it certifies that it employs a filtering or blocking system on one or more of its computers. It also requires the library to notify the FCC within ten days after changing or terminating such a system. The determination of what shall be considered inappropriate for minors is to be made by the appropriate school, school board, library, or other responsible authority, without Federal interference.

The text of the Safe Schools Internet Act of 1999 is set forth at Appendix 9.

CHAPTER 9:

EDUCATION

Restrictions on Expression in Public Schools

The government's goal in providing education and training to the nation's youth has, at times, required restriction upon expression, which has generally been upheld by the Supreme Court unless the restriction clearly exceeded its purpose. Nevertheless, in a variety of decisions, as set forth below, the Court has established that public school students, including minors, are entitled to some measure of constitutional protection.

Tinker v. Des Moines Independent Community School District

In *Tinker v. Des Moines Independent Community School District*, 393 U.S. 503 (1969), high school principals had banned students from wearing black armbands as a symbol of protest against the Vietnam War. In reversing the lower court's refusal to reinstate students who had been suspended for violating the ban, the Court formulated a balancing test which required that restriction on expression by school authorities is only permissible to prevent disruption of educational discipline:

"First Amendment rights, applied in light of the special characteristics of the school environment, are available to teachers and students. It can hardly be argued that either students or teachers shed their constitutional rights to freedom of speech or expression at the school house gate . . . On the other hand, the Court has repeatedly emphasized the need for affirming the comprehensive authority of the States and of school officials, consistent with fundamental constitutional . . . In order for the State in the person of school officials to justify prohibition of a particular expression of opinion, it must be able to show that its action was caused by something more than a mere desire to avoid the discomfort and unpleasantness that always accompany an unpopular viewpoint. Certainly where there is no finding and no showing that engaging in the forbidden conduct would materially and substantially interfere with the requirements of appropriate discipline in the operation of the school,' the prohibition cannot be sustained."

Thus, *Tinker* stands for the proposition that students may express their opinions orally and in writing, as long as they do so in a way that does not "materially and substantially" disrupt school activities.

Healy v. James

In *Healy v. James*, 408 U.S. 169 (1972), the Court reaffirmed its decision in *Tinker* in ruling that the withholding of recognition of a student organization by a public college administration violated the students' right of association. The Court ruled that denial of recognition was unconstitutional if it was based on the organization's philosophy, their affiliation with the national SDS organization, or a generalized fear of disruption without any basis. The Court held:

> "[W]here state-operated educational institutions are involved, this Court has long recognized . . . the comprehensive authority of the States and of school officials . . . to prescribe and control conduct in the schools . . . Yet, the precedents of this Court leave no room for the view that, because of the acknowledged need for order, First Amendment protections should apply with less force on college campuses than in the community at large . . . [T]he vigilant protection of constitutional freedoms is nowhere more vital than in the community of American schools.

The Court further held that a college may impose reasonable regulations to maintain order so that learning may take place, and it may require each organization to affirm its willingness to adhere to reasonable campus law as a prerequisite to recognition.

Hazelwood School District v. Kuhlmeier

In *Hazelwood School Dist. v. Kuhlmeier*, 484 U.S. 260 (1988), the Court distinguished *Tinker*, holding that editorial control and censorship of a student newspaper sponsored by a public high school need only be "reasonably related to legitimate pedagogical concerns."

The principal's decisions to prohibit publication of an article describing student pregnancy in a manner believed inappropriate for younger students, and another article on divorce critical of a named parent, were thus upheld.

The Court ruled:

> "The question whether the First Amendment requires a school to tolerate particular student speech—the question that we addressed in *Tinker*— is different from the question [in *Hazelwood*] whether the First Amendment requires a school affirmatively to promote particular student speech."

Thus, *Hazelwood* stands for the proposition that restrictions on school-sponsored speech—which would include school sponsored activities such as plays, publications, art shows, and other expressive activities that students, parents and the public might reasonably believe are supported by the school—are constitutional provided there is a reasonable basis.

Hate Speech on Campus

In recent years, college campuses have been the setting for violent and abusive attacks on minority groups. Many school administrators have responded to this problem by adopting codes or policies prohibiting speech that offends any group based on race, gender, ethnicity, religion or sexual orientation.

Opponents of such speech codes argue that the First Amendment protects speech no matter how offensive the content. They further argue that restrictions on speech by public colleges amounts to government censorship. They propose that offensive speech should instead be countered by more speech which promotes the opposite viewpoint, in order to provide open debate and enlightenment.

CHAPTER 10:

HATE SPEECH

In General

Another area of First Amendment controversy involves the right to engage in "hate speech," such as that which may be expected from such adversarial groups as the Ku Klux Klan or Neo-Nazi type groups. Advocates for free speech argue that the First Amendment protects all speech, regardless of whether it is offensive, arguing that any infringement of free speech rights will endanger the rights of all people, and will give the government the right to decide which opinions ought to be expressed and which should be censored.

Nevertheless, freedom of speech does not permit *conduct* which intimidates, harasses or threatens another, even if that conduct is carried out through the use of words. For example, obscene telephone calls would not be protected speech.

The Supreme Court has held that non-verbal symbols of expression—which would include symbols of hate such as swastikas or burning crosses—are constitutionally protected because they are "closely akin to "pure speech." Nevertheless, the First Amendment does not protect the use of non-verbal symbols used to damage or desecrate private property.

Group Libel

In *Beauharnais v. Illinois*, 343 U.S. 250 (1952), the Supreme Court upheld a state group libel law which made it unlawful to defame a race or class of people. The defendant, a white supremacist, distributed a leaflet which called for action to keep African Americans out of white neighborhoods. The Court reasoned that if libel of an individual was a criminal act not entitled to First Amendment protection, then there is no good reason to deny a state the power to punish the same speech when it is directed at a defined group.

The *Beauharnais* holding was subsequently weakened by the decision in *In R. A. V. v. City of St. Paul*, 112 S. Ct. 2538 (1992), in which the Court struck down a hate crimes ordinance construed by the state courts to apply only to the use of "fighting words." Because the ordinance proscribed only those fighting words that would arouse anger, alarm, or resentment in others on the basis of "race, color, creed, religion, or gender," and did not ban other possible bases, such as homosexuality or political affiliation, it was invalidated for content discrimination.

The Hate Crimes Prevention Act of 1999 (H.R. 1082)

The Hate Crimes Prevention Act of 1999 was introduced in the House of Representatives on March 11, 1999 by Representative John Conyers, and was referred to the Subcommittee on Crime on April 1, 1999.

The Act prohibits anyone from willfully causing bodily injury to any person or, through the use of fire, a firearm, or an explosive device, attempts to cause bodily injury to any person, because of the actual or perceived race, color, religion, or national origin of that person.

Congress determined that the incidence of violence motivated by "hate" directed at the defined groups is divisive, poses a serious national problem, disrupts the tranquility and safety of communities, and negatively impacts interstate commerce in the manner set forth in the Act.

Congress concluded that existing Federal law was inadequate to address the problem and, although state and local jurisdictions will continue to prosecute the vast majority of bias-related crimes, Federal jurisdiction is necessary to supplement state and local jurisdiction and ensure that justice is achieved in each case.

Free speech proponents, such as the ACLU, although generally in favor of the Act's prohibition on bias-related violence, have expressed concerns that the Act could have a chilling effect on constitutionally protected speech. Thus, they have urged Congress to amend the Act by providing that evidence of a defendant's "mere abstract beliefs," or "mere membership in an organization" will not be admissible to establish any element of an offense under the Act.

Although the Act, on its face, seeks only to punish the "conduct" of selecting another person for violence because of his or her race, color, national origin, religion, gender, sexual orientation, or disability, there is concern that, in proving the intentional conduct, the prosecution will bring in evidence of the defendant's racial bigotry or association with hate groups.

For example, the prosecutor may introduce racial or other bigoted epithets directed toward the victim by the defendant. Thus, the finder of fact may conclude that the speech-related evidence is a proper basis for proving the intentional selection element of the offense, whether or not it was related to the chain of events leading to the violence. Further, associating the defendant with a particular "hate group" may serve to convict the defendant on a "guilt by association" type theory.

The proposed amendment to the Act, they argue, will reduce or eliminate the possibility that the government could obtain a criminal conviction on the basis of evidence of speech-related activities that had no role in the chain of events that led to any alleged violent act proscribed by the statute.

The text of the Hate Crimes Prevention Act of 1999 is set forth at Appendix 10.

APPENDICES

APPENDIX 1:

THE FIRST AMENDMENT

Congress shall make no law respecting an establishment of religion, or prohibiting the free exercise thereof; or abridging the freedom of speech, or of the press; or the right of the people peaceably to assemble, and to petition the government for a redress of grievances.

APPENDIX 2:

THE FOURTEENTH AMENDMENT

All persons born or naturalized in the United States, and subject to the jurisdiction thereof, are citizens of the United States and of the state wherein they reside. No state shall make or enforce any law which shall abridge the privileges or immunities of citizens of the United States; nor shall any state deprive any person of life, liberty, or property, without due process of law; nor deny to any person within its jurisdiction the equal protection of the laws.

DIRECTORY OF ORGANIZATIONS CONCERNED WITH FIRST AMENDMENT ISSUES

ORGANIZATION	ADDRESS	TELEPHONE NUMBER	FAX NUMBER	E-MAIL	WEBSITE
American Booksellers Foundation for Free Expression	139 Fulton Street, Suite 302, New York, NY 10038	212-587-4205	212-587-2436	ABFFE @bookweb. org	http://www .bookweb. org/orgs/ realted/ abffe
The American Civil Liberties Union (ACLU) - National Office	125 Broad Street, 18th Floor, New York, NY 10004	212-549-2500	212-549-2646	infoaclu @aclu.org	http://www. aclu.org/
The American Civil Liberties Union (ACLU) of Ohio	1266 West 6th Street, 2nd Floor Cleveland, Ohio 44113	216-781-6276	N/A	N/A	http://www. en.com/users /aclucle
The American Civil Liberties Union (ACLU) of Oregon	P.O. Box 40585, Portland, Oregon 97240	503-227-6928	503-227-6948	info @aclu-or.org	http://www. acluor.org/ aclu
The American Civil Liberties Union (ACLU) of Wisconsin	207 E. Buffalo Street, Suite 325, Milwaukee, Wisconsin 53202-5712	414-272-4032	414-272-0182	acluwisc @mail. execpc.com	URL http://www. aclu-wi.org/
Americans for Radio Diversity	N/A	N/A	N/A	ard @radparker. com	http://www. radiodiversity. com/
Boston Coalition for Freedom of Expression	354 Congress Street Boston, Massachusetts 02210	617-497-7193	617-451-2910	kyp @inrranet. com	http://www. ultranet.com/ ~kyp/bcfe. html

ORGANIZATION	ADDRESS	TELEPHONE NUMBER	FAX NUMBER	E-MAIL	WEBSITE
Brechner Center for Freedom of Information	University of Florida College of Journalism and Communications 3208 Weimer Hall, Gainesville, Florida 32611	352-392-2273	N/A	N/A	http://www.jou.ufl.edu/brechner/brochure.htm
California Anti-SLAPP Project	1611 Telegraph Avenue, Suite 1200 Oakland, California 94612	510-835-0850	510-465-1985	casp @sirius.com	http://www.sirius.com/~casp/welcome.html
California First Amendment Coalition	2701 Cottage Way Sacramento, California 95825-1226	916-974-8888	916-974-8880	cfac @cfac. org	http://www.cfac.org/ Center for Democracy and Technology
Citizens Internet Empowerment Coalition	1001 G Street N.W., Suite 700 East, Washington, D.C. 20001	202-637-9800	202-637-0968	ciec @cdt. org	http://www.cdt.org/ciec/
Comic Book Legal Defense Fund	P.O. Box 693, Northampton, MA 01061	1-800-99-CBLDF	413-582-9046	cbldf @codexx. com	http://www.edgeglobal.com/cbldf/
Committee Against Censorship - National Council of Teachers of English	1111 West Kenyon, Urbana, Illinois 61801	715-328-3870	715-328-0977	nctecsuh @vmd.cso.uiuc.edu	N/A
Committee to Protect Journalists	330 Seventh Avenue, New York, NY 10001	212-465-1004	212-465-9568	info@cpj.org	http://www.cpj.org/
Digital Freedom Network	190 Main Street, Hackensack, New Jersey 07601	201-928-4378	201-907-5165	bwong @corp.idt.net	http://www.dfn.org/

ORGANIZATION	ADDRESS	TELEPHONE NUMBER	FAX NUMBER	E-MAIL	WEBSITE
The Electronic Frontier Foundation	1667 K Street N.W., Suite 801, Washington, D.C. 20006	202-861-7700	202 861-1258	eff@eff.org	http://www.eff.org/
Electronic Frontiers of Florida	2502 W. Azeele Street, Tampa, Florida 33609	813-348-4220	813-870-0824	info @efflorida. org	http://www.efflorida.org/
Electronic Privacy Information Center	666 Pennsylvania Avenue S.E., Suite 301, Washington, D.C. 20003	202-544- 9240	202-547-5482	info @epic.org	http:// epic.org
Feminists for Free Expression	2525 Times Square Station, New York, New York 10108	212-702-6292	212-702-6277	freedom @well.com	http://www.well.com/ user/freedom/
First Amendment Foundation	1313 West 8th Street, Suite 313, Los Angeles, California 90017	213-484-6661	213-484- 0266	NCARL @aol.com	http://www.thefirstamend-ment.org
First Amendment Lawyers Association	N/A	N/A	N/A	N/A	http://www.mooneylaw.com/FALA/ PAGES/ ROSTER. HTML
The First Amendment Project	1736 Franklin Street, Eighth Floor Oakland, CA 94612	510-208-7744	510-465-6248	fap @well. com	www.well.com/user/ fap/
Florida Coalition Against Censorship	310 Michigan Avenue, Lynn Haven, Florida 32444-1428	904-265-6438	904-271- 3136	pipking @mail.firn.edu	http://www.afn.org/

ORGANIZATION	ADDRESS	TELEPHONE NUMBER	FAX NUMBER	E-MAIL	WEBSITE
Foodspeak Coalition for Free Speech	1875 Connecticut Avenue N.W., Suite 300, Washington, D.C. 20009	202-332-9110	202-265-4954	foodspeak @cspinet.org	http://www. cspinet.org/ foodspeak/
Free Radio Berkeley	1442 A Walnut Street, Berkeley, California 94709	510-594-8082	N/A	frbspd @crl.com	http://www. freeradio. org
Free Expression Network	N/A	N/A	N/A	webmaster @freeexpres sion.org	http://www. freeexpression .org/
The Freedom Forum First Amendment Center	1207 18th Avenue South, Nashville, Tennessee 37212	615-321-9588	615-321-9599	web@fac.org	http://www. freedomforum .org/ first/ welcome.asp
Freedom of Information Committee	11600 Sunrise Valley Drive, Reston, Virginia 22091	703-648-1145	703-620-4557	flandon @infi.net	N/A
The Freedom of Information Foundation of Texas	9000 N. Broadway, Oklahoma City, Oklahoma 73125	405-475-3384	405-325-3183	globow @aol.com	http://www. reporters. net/foift
Freedom to Read Committee	1718 Connecticut Avenue N.W., Washington, D.C. 20009-1148	202-232-3335	202-745-0694	N/A	N/A
Freedom to Read Foundation	50 East Huron Street, Chicago, Illinois 60611-2795	312-944-6780	312-440-9374	ftrf@ala.org	http://www. ala.org/ alaorg/ oif/ftrf_home. htm
The Fund for Constitutional Government	122 Maryland Avenue N.E., Washington, D.C. 20002	202-546-3799	202-543-3156	FunConGov @aol.com	N/A

ORGANIZATION	ADDRESS	TELEPHONE NUMBER	FAX NUMBER	E-MAIL	WEBSITE
Georgia First Amendment Foundation	990 Edgewood Avenue N.E., Atlanta, Georgia 30307	404-577-7103	404-525-4570	gfaf @mindspring. com	http://www mindspring. com/~gfaf/
Human Rights Watch Fund for Free Expression	485 Fifth Avenue, New York, New York 10017-6104	212-972-8400	212-986-3357	hrwnyc @hrw.org	gopher:// humanrights. org:5000/
Individual Rights Foundation	Box 67398, Los Angeles, California 9006-9507	310-843-3699	310-843-3629	76042.3271 @compu-serve.com	N/A
Intellectual Freedom Action Network	50 East Huron Street Chicago, Illinois 60611	1-800-545-2433	312-280-4227	oif@ala.org	http://www. ala.org/ alaorg/ oif/ifan_html
The Internet Users Consortium	7031 E. Camelback, Suite 102-515, Scottsdale, Arizona 85251	602-874-1492	602-970- 3689	molsen @indirect. com	http://www. indirect.com
Justice on Campus	N/A	N/A	N/A	joc @joc.mit.edu	http:// joc.mit.edu/
Libraries for the Future	521 Fifth Avenue, Suite 1612, New York, NY 10175-1699	212-682-7446	212-682-7657	lff @inch.com	http:// www.inch. com/~lff/
The Literary Network	154 Christopher Street, New York, NY 10014	212-741-9110	212-741-9112	anneburt @tmn.com	N/A
The Media Coalition Inc.	139 Fulton Street, Suite 302, New York, NY 10038	212-587-4025	212-587-2436	Media-coalition @media-coalition.org	N/A

ORGANIZATION	ADDRESS	TELEPHONE NUMBER	FAX NUMBER	E-MAIL	WEBSITE
The Media Institute	1000 Potomac Street N.W., Suite 301, Washington, D.C. 20007	202-298-7512	202-337-7092	tmi @clark.net	http://www. mediainst. org
National Association of Scholars	575 Ewing Street, Princeton, New Jersey 08540	609-683-7878	609-683-0316	nas@nas.org	http://www. nas.org/
National Campaign for Freedom of Expression	918 F Street NW Washington, D.C. 20004	202-393-2787	202-347-7376	ncfe @artswire. org	http://www. artswire.org/ ncfe/
National Coalition Against Censorship	275 Seventh Avenue, New York, NY 10001	212-807-6222	212-807-6245	ncac @netcom. com	http://www. ncac.org/
National Freedom of Information Coalition	400 South Record Street, Sixth Floor, Dallas, Texas 75202	214-977-6658	214-977-6666	foift @airmail.net	http://www. reporters. net/nfoic/
NorthWest Feminists Anti-Censorship Taskforce	12345 Lake City Way N.E., Seattle, Washington 98125	206-292-1159	206-367-7756	nw-fact @aa.net	http://www. aa.net/ ~nw-fact/
Office for Intellectual Freedom	50 East Huron Street, Chicago, Illinois 60611-2795	312-944-6780	312-440-9374	oif@ala.org	http://www. ala.org/oif. html
PEN Freedom to Write Committee	568 Broadway, New York, New York 10012-3225	212-334-1660	212-334-2181	pen @echonyc. com	http://www. pen.org/
People for the American Way	2000 M Street N.W., Suite 400, Washington, D.C. 20036	202-467-4999	202-293-2672	pfaw @pfaw.org	http://www. pfaw.org/

ORGANIZATION	ADDRESS	TELEPHONE NUMBER	FAX NUMBER	E-MAIL	WEBSITE
Reporters Committee for Freedom of the Press	1101 Wilson Blvd., Suite 1910, Arlington, Virginia 22209-2248	703-807-2100	703-807-2109	rcfp @rcfp.com	http://www. rcfp.org/rcfp/
Rock Out Censorship	P.O.Box 147, Jewett, Ohio 43986	614-946-6535	614-946-6535	roc @theroc.org	http://www. theroc.org/
The Society for Electronic Access	P.O.Box 7081, New York, NY 10116-7081	212-592-3801	N/A	clay@sea.org	http://www. sea.org/
Society of Professional Journalists	16 South Jackson Street, Greencastle, Indiana 46135-1514	317-653-3333	317-653- 4631	quillnet @link2000. net	http://spj.org/
Student Press Law Center	1101 Wilson Blvd, Suite 1910, Arlington, VA 22209-2248	703-807-1904	N/A	splc @splc.org	http://www. splc.org/
Thomas Jefferson Center for the Protection of Free Expression	400 Peter Jefferson Place Charlottesville, Virginia 22901	804-295-4784	804-295-3621	jwheeler @igc.apc.org	http://www. tjcenter.org
Voters Telecommunications Watch	233 Court Street, Suite 2 Brooklyn, New York 11201	718-596-2851	N/A	shabbir @panix.com	http://www. vtw.org/

THE FLAG PROTECTION ACT OF 1999
H.R.1081

SPONSOR: Rep Boucher, Rick (introduced 03/11/99)

SUMMARY (AS INTRODUCED): The Flag Protection Act of 1999 amends the Federal criminal code to revise provisions regarding desecration of the flag to set penalties with respect to persons who: (1) destroy or damage a U.S. flag with intent to provoke, and in circumstances reasonably likely to produce, imminent violence or a breach of the peace; (2) steal or knowingly convert to their use, or the use of another, a U.S. flag belonging to the United States and intentionally destroy or damage that flag; and (3) within any lands reserved for the use of the United States, or under the exclusive or concurrent jurisdiction thereof, steal or knowingly convert to their use, or the use of another, a U.S. flag belonging to another person and intentionally destroy or damage that flag.

[The Act] Expresses the sense of the Congress that the States should enact prohibitions similar to the provisions of this Act.

IN THE HOUSE OF REPRESENTATIVES

March 11, 1999

Mr. BOUCHER (for himself, Mr. GILCHREST, Mr. PETRI, Mr. JEFFERSON, Mr. TANNER, Mr. PRICE of North Carolina, and Mr. FROST) introduced the following bill; which was referred to the Committee on the Judiciary

A BILL

To provide for protection of the flag of the United States.

Be it enacted by the Senate and House of Representatives of the United States of America in Congress assembled,

SECTION 1. SHORT TITLE.

This Act may be cited as the 'Flag Protection Act of 1999'.

SECTION 2. PROTECTION OF THE FLAG OF THE UNITED STATES.

(a) IN GENERAL—Section 700 of title 18, United States Code, is amended to read as follows:

'Sec. 700. Protection of the flag of the United States

(a) ACTIONS PROMOTING VIOLENCE—Any person who destroys or damages a flag of the United States with intent to provoke imminent violence or a breach of the peace, and in circumstances reasonably likely to produce imminent violence or a breach of the peace, shall be fined under this title or imprisoned not more than one year, or both.

(b) DAMAGING A FLAG BELONGING TO THE UNITED STATES—Any person who steals or knowingly converts to his or her use, or to the use of another, a flag of the United States belonging to the United States and intentionally destroys or damages that flag shall be fined under this title or imprisoned not more than two years, or both.

(c) DAMAGING A FLAG OF ANOTHER ON FEDERAL LAND—Any person who, within any lands reserved for the use of the United States, or under the exclusive or concurrent jurisdiction thereof, steals or knowingly converts to his or her use, or to the use of another, a flag of the United States belonging to another person and intentionally destroys or damages that flag shall be fined under this title or imprisoned not more than two years, or both.

(d) CONSTRUCTION—Nothing in this section shall be construed as indicating an intent on the part of Congress to deprive any State, territory, possession, or the Commonwealth of Puerto Rico of jurisdiction over any offense over which it would have jurisdiction in the absence of this section.

(e) DEFINITION—As used in this section, the term 'flag of the United States' means any flag of the United States, or any part thereof, made of any substance, of any size, in a form that is commonly displayed as a flag and would taken to be a flag by the reasonable observer.'.

(b) CLERICAL AMENDMENT—The table of sections for chapter 33 of title 18, United States Code, is amended by striking out the item relating to section 700 and inserting in lieu thereof the following new item:

700. Protection of the flag of the United States.'.

SECTION 3. SENSE OF CONGRESS.

It is the sense of the Congress that the States should enact prohibitions similar to the provisions of this Act in an order to provide the maximum protection to the flag of the United States.

106th CONGRESS

1st Session

HOUSE ACTIONS:

March 11, 1999: Referred to the House Committee on the Judiciary.

APPENDIX 5:

S.J. RES 14 - JOINT RESOLUTION PROPOSING A CONSTITUTIONAL AMENDMENT TO DECLARE THAT CONGRESS HAS THE POWER TO PROHIBIT PHYSICAL DESECRATION OF THE FLAG

SPONSOR: Sen Hatch, Orrin G. (introduced 03/17/99)

SUMMARY (AS INTRODUCED): Constitutional Amendment - Declares that Congress shall have power to prohibit the physical desecration of the U.S. flag.

Proposing an amendment to the Constitution of the United States authorizing Congress to prohibit the physical desecration of the flag of the United States.

IN THE SENATE OF THE UNITED STATES

March 17, 1999

Mr. HATCH (for himself, Mr. CLELAND, Mr. ABRAHAM, Mr. AL-LARD, Mr. ASHCROFT, Mr. BAUCUS, Mr. BOND, Mr. BREAUX, Mr. BROWNBACK, Mr. BUNNING, Mr. BURNS, Mr. CAMPBELL, Ms. COLLINS, Mr. COVERDELL, Mr. CRAIG, Mr. CRAPO, Mr. DEWINE, Mr. DOMENICI, Mr. ENZI, Mrs. FEINSTEIN, Mr. FITZGERALD, Mr. FRIST, Mr. GORTON, Mr. GRAHAM, Mr. GRAMM, Mr. GRAMS, Mr. GRASSLEY, Mr. GREGG, Mr. HAGEL, Mr. HELMS, Mr. HOLLINGS, Mr. HUTCHINSON, Mrs. HUTCHISON, Mr. INHOFE, Mr. JOHNSON, Mr. KYL, Mrs. LINCOLN, Mr. LOTT, Mr. LUGAR, Mr. MACK, Mr. MCCAIN, Mr. MURKOWSKI, Mr. NICKLES, Mr. REID, Mr. ROBERTS, Mr. ROTH, Mr. SANTORUM, Mr. SESSIONS, Mr. SHELBY, Mr. SMITH of New Hampshire, Ms. SNOWE, Mr. SPECTER, Mr. STEVENS, Mr. THOMAS, Mr. THOMPSON, Mr. THURMOND, and Mr. WARNER, and Mr. VOINOVICH) introduced the following joint resolution; which was read twice and referred to the Committee on the Judiciary:

JOINT RESOLUTION

Proposing an amendment to the Constitution of the United States authorizing Congress to prohibit the physical desecration of the flag of the United States.

Resolved by the Senate and House of Representatives of the United States of America in Congress assembled (two-thirds of each House concurring therein), That the following article is proposed as an amendment to the

Constitution of the United States, which shall be valid to all intents and purposes as part of the Constitution when ratified by the legislatures of three-fourths of the several States within 7 years after the date of its submission for ratification:

ARTICLE —

"The Congress shall have power to prohibit the physical desecration of the flag of the United States."

Calendar No. 98

106th CONGRESS

1st Session

SENATE ACTIONS:

March 17, 1999: Read twice and referred to the Committee on Judiciary.

March 23, 1999: Referred to Subcommittee on Constitution, Federalism, Property.

April 21, 1999: Subcommittee on Constitution, Federalism, Property. Approved for full committee consideration without amendment favorably.

April 20, 1999: Committee on Judiciary. Hearings held.

April 29, 1999: Committee on Judiciary. Ordered to be reported without amendment favorably.

April 29, 1999: Committee on Judiciary. Reported to Senate by Senator Hatch without amendment. Without written report.

TEXT OF THE ACLU STATEMENT IN OPPOSITION
TO FLAG DESECRATION LEGISLATION

Before the United States Senate Constitution, Federalism and Property Rights Subcommittee of the Senate Judiciary Committee Hearing on "The Tradition and Importance of Protecting the United States Flag."

March 25, 1998

Mr. Chairman and Members of the Subcommittee:

On behalf of the American Civil Liberties Union, thank you for the opportunity to submit this statement in opposition to S.J. Res. 14, the proposed constitutional amendment to ban flag desecration. More than a statement of opposition, this is a statement in support of one of the greatest freedoms embodied in the Constitution: the First Amendment, within it, the freedom to protest and criticize the government.

The ACLU continues to oppose a constitutional amendment to "protect the flag" for the same reasons we opposed such an amendment when it was first introduced in 1989, and again in 1990: It would do irreparable harm to the First Amendment and would undermine the very principles for which the American flag stands.

For two centuries, the Bill of Rights has stood as a beacon of liberty, permitting the freest expression of political and other views of any country in the world. Our forebears fought a revolution and a Civil War to make this the land of freedom and liberty. The experience from our history has taught us that our freedoms are very delicate and must be shielded from all intrusions. "[I]t is proper to take alarm at the first experiment on our liberties," advised James Madison, who was the principal author of the Constitution and the Bill of Rights. That alarm is fully justified by the flag desecration amendment.

This proposed constitutional amendment to give Congress the power to ban flag desecration would mark the first time ever in our nation's history that Congress has amended the Bill of Rights to remove a fundamental individual right. In fact, in our history, there have been over 7,000 proposed constitutional amendments, and only 27 successful amendments.

James Madison said that the Constitution should only be amended on "great and extraordinary occasions." It is incumbent on this committee to ask: Is this a "great and extraordinary occasion?" According to a July, 1997

Freedom Forum poll, less than half of the respondents supported the proposed flag amendment, and a majority (70%) opposed it after learning that it would be the first time First Amendment freedoms would be amended.

The First Amendment has survived the Civil War, the Cold War, presidential assassinations, and the turbulent Civil Rights era of the 1960's. This Committee is now considering a precedent-shattering amendment, and for what purpose? Far from being a national epidemic, published reports indicate that burning incidents have occurred, on average, less than five times per year since *Texas v. Johnson*, the 1990 flag decision in which the Supreme Court struck down flag desecration laws.

Further, most cases of flag burning remain punishable without resort to a constitutional amendment. Mutilation or burning of flags belonging to the government or to non-consenting individuals are typically punishable under public burning, larceny or destruction of public or private property statutes.

There is a distinct difference between real patriotism and forced patriotism. We abhor flag burning because the flag represents what is great and worth fighting for about America. For the same reason, we also abhor the shredding of the Bill of Rights that this amendment represents. Indeed, it is sadly ironic that, as two Hong Kong residents presently await trial for the crime of altering Chinese and Hong Kong flags, this Committee would consider following China's lead on the right to free speech and democratic protest.

Flag burning may well be a deeply offensive form of political protest, but it is political nonetheless and, as such, it is rightly entitled to the highest form of First Amendment protections. There are many forms of expression that many would find just as offensive. For instance, cross burnings, swastikas, and book burnings are deeply offensive to many. Would the enactment of this Amendment mean that other proposed Amendments would quickly follow? And, if we move to amend the constitution to make sure that the public is not offended, what sort of country would we find ourselves living in? Flag burning today, what will we ban tomorrow?

Furthermore, what sort of "physical desecration" would the flag amendment allow Congress to prohibit? Would it prohibit American flag lapel pins or T-shirts? The truth is, law enforcement and prosecutors would only arrest and prosecute uses of the flag that they consider "desecration." A new flag law would likely be enforced only to repress political protest that the government considers "disrespectful." These laws would strike at the content of the message of the "desecrator," exactly what the First Amendment is meant to protect.

Speech—verbal or symbolic—can be offensive and provocative. But freedom cannot survive if exceptions are made every time someone in power feels offended or provoked. If we allow that, our right to free speech will depend on what the President or Congress finds acceptable. That is precisely what the First Amendment was designed to prevent. This is not a conservative or liberal issue. It goes to the heart of what this country and the flag stand for.

When the U.S. Supreme Court upheld the First Amendment right to desecrate the flag as a form of political protest, the majority decision included noted conservatives as well as liberals. The Court understood that the First Amendment is indivisible and that what the flag stands for encompasses the freedom to defile it.

Patriotism is something Americans feel because we are proud of our country. We respect our flag because we are proud to be Americans, not because of some law that forces us to pledge allegiance or suffer the consequences. We should be more worried about the desecration of the Bill of Rights contemplated here today, then about the few, isolated acts by a few extremists.

It is important to note that the First Amendment protects the full range of speech, popular and unpopular alike. In 1984, the Supreme Court said: "[T]he First Amendment presupposes that the freedom to speak one's mind is not only an aspect of individual liberty—and thus a good unto itself—but also is essential to the common quest for truth and the vitality of society as a whole." *(City Council of Los Angeles v. Taxpayers for Vincent.)*

The ACLU urges the Senate Constitution, Federalism and Property Rights Subcommittee of the Senate Judiciary Committee to reject this Amendment, and to save the Bill of Rights of our Constitution, for which our flag has stood so proudly for over 200 years. Thank you.

Solange E. Bitol, Legislative Counsel

ACLU Washington National Office

THE CHILD PORNOGRAPHY PROTECTION ACT OF 1996

PUBLIC LAW 104-208 (September 30, 1996)

Section 2252A. CERTAIN ACTIVITIES RELATING TO MATERIAL CONSTITUTING OR CONTAINING CHILD PORNOGRAPHY

(a) Any person who—

(1) knowingly mails, or transports or ships in interstate or foreign commerce by any means, including by computer, any child pornography;

(2) knowingly receives or distributes—

(A) any child pornography that has been mailed, or shipped or transported in interstate or foreign commerce by any means, including by computer; or

(B) any material that contains child pornography that has been mailed, or shipped or transported in interstate or foreign commerce by any means, including by computer;

(3) knowingly reproduces any child pornography for distribution through the mails, or in interstate or foreign commerce by any means, including by computer;

(4) either—

(A) in the special maritime and territorial jurisdiction of the United States, or on any land or building owned by, leased to, or otherwise used by or under the control of the United States Government, or in the Indian country (as defined in section 1151), knowingly sells or possesses with the intent to sell any child pornography; or

(B) knowingly sells or possesses with the intent to sell any child pornography that has been mailed, or shipped or transported in interstate or foreign commerce by any means, including by computer, or that was produced using materials that have been mailed, or shipped or transported in interstate or foreign commerce by any means, including by computer; or

(5) either—

(A) in the special maritime and territorial jurisdiction of the United States, or on any land or building owned by, leased to, or otherwise used by or under the control of the United States Government, or in the Indian country (as defined in section 1151), knowingly possesses any book, magazine, periodical, film, videotape, computer disk, or any other material that contains 3 or more images of child pornography; or

(B) knowingly possesses any book, magazine, periodical, film, videotape, computer disk, or any other material that contains 3 or more images of child pornography that has been mailed, or shipped or transported in interstate or foreign commerce by any means, including by computer, or that was produced using materials that have been mailed, or shipped or transported in interstate or foreign commerce by any means, including by computer, shall be punished as provided in subsection (b).

(b)(1) Whoever violates, or attempts or conspires to violate, paragraphs (1), (2), (3), or (4) of subsection (a) shall be fined under this title or imprisoned not more than 15 years, or both, but, if such person has a prior conviction under this chapter or chapter 109A, or under the laws of any State relating to aggravated sexual abuse, sexual abuse, or abusive sexual conduct involving a minor or ward, or the production, possession, receipt, mailing, sale, distribution, shipment, or transportation of child pornography, such person shall be fined under this title and imprisoned for not less than 5 years nor more than 30 years.

(b)(2) Whoever violates, or attempts or conspires to violate, subsection (a)(5) shall be fined under this title or imprisoned not more than 5 years, or both, but, if such person has a prior conviction under this chapter or chapter 109A, or under the laws of any State relating to the possession of child pornography, such person shall be fined under this title and imprisoned for not less than 2 years nor more than 10 years.

(c) It shall be an affirmative defense to a charge of violating paragraphs (1), (2), (3), or (4) of subsection (a) that—

(1) the alleged child pornography was produced using an actual person or persons engaging in sexually explicit conduct;

(2) each such person was an adult at the time the material was produced; and

(3) the defendant did not advertise, promote, present, describe, or distribute the material in such a manner as to

convey the impression that it is or contains a visual depiction of a minor engaging in sexually explicit conduct.

(b) TECHNICAL AMENDMENT—The table of sections for chapter 110 of title 18, United States Code, is amended by adding after the item relating to section 2252 the following: 2252A. Certain activities relating to material constituting or containing child pornography.'

APPENDIX 8:

THE CHILD ONLINE PROTECTION ACT OF 1998
(H.R.3783)

AN ACT

To amend the Communications Act of 1934 to require persons who are engaged in the business of distributing, by means of the World Wide Web, material that is harmful to minors to restrict access to such material by minors, and for other purposes.

Be it enacted by the Senate and House of Representatives of the United States of America in Congress assembled,

SECTION 1. SHORT TITLE.

This Act may be cited as the 'Child Online Protection Act'.

TITLE I—PROTECTION FROM MATERIAL THAT IS HARMFUL TO MINORS

SECTION 101. CONGRESSIONAL FINDINGS.

The Congress finds that—

(1) while custody, care, and nurture of the child resides first with the parent, the widespread availability of the Internet presents opportunities for minors to access materials through the World Wide Web in a manner that can frustrate parental supervision or control;

(2) the protection of the physical and psychological well-being of minors by shielding them from materials that are harmful to them is a compelling governmental interest;

(3) to date, while the industry has developed innovative ways to help parents and educators restrict material that is harmful to minors through parental control protections and self-regulation, such efforts have not provided a national solution to the problem of minors accessing harmful material on the World Wide Web;

(4) a prohibition on the distribution of material harmful to minors, combined with legitimate defenses, is currently the most effective and least restrictive means by which to satisfy the compelling government interest; and

(5) notwithstanding the existence of protections that limit the distribution over the World Wide Web of material that is harmful to minors, parents, educators, and industry must continue efforts to find ways to protect children from being exposed to harmful material found on the Internet.

SECTION 102. REQUIREMENT TO RESTRICT ACCESS BY MINORS TO MATERIALS COMMERCIALLY DISTRIBUTED BY MEANS OF THE WORLD WIDE WEB THAT ARE HARMFUL TO MINORS.

Part I of title II of the Communications Act of 1934 (47 U.S.C. 201 et seq.) is amended by adding at the end the following new section:

SECTION 231. RESTRICTION OF ACCESS BY MINORS TO MATERIALS COMMERCIALLY DISTRIBUTED BY MEANS OF WORLD WIDE WEB THAT ARE HARMFUL TO MINORS.

(a) REQUIREMENT TO RESTRICT ACCESS—

(1) PROHIBITED CONDUCT—Whoever knowingly and with knowledge of the character of the material, in interstate or foreign commerce by means of the World Wide Web, makes any communication for commercial purposes that is available to any minor and that includes any material that is harmful to minors shall be fined not more than $50,000, imprisoned not more than 6 months, or both.

(2) INTENTIONAL VIOLATIONS—In addition to the penalties under paragraph (1), whoever intentionally violates such paragraph shall be subject to a fine of not more than $50,000 for each violation. For purposes of this paragraph, each day of violation shall constitute a separate violation.

(3) CIVIL PENALTY—In addition to the penalties under paragraphs (1) and (2), whoever violates paragraph (1) shall be subject to a civil penalty of not more than $50,000 for each violation. For purposes of this paragraph, each day of violation shall constitute a separate violation.

(b) INAPPLICABILITY OF CARRIERS AND OTHER SERVICE PROVIDERS—For purposes of subsection (a), a person shall not be considered to make any communication for commercial purposes to the extent that such person is—

(1) a telecommunications carrier engaged in the provision of a telecommunications service;

(2) a person engaged in the business of providing an Internet access service;

(3) a person engaged in the business of providing an Internet information location tool; or

(4) similarly engaged in the transmission, storage, retrieval, hosting, formatting, or translation (or any combination thereof) of a communication made by another person, without selection or alteration of the content of the communication, except that such person's deletion of a particular communication or material made by another person in a manner consistent with subsection (c) or section 230 shall not constitute such selection or alteration of the content of the communication.

(c) AFFIRMATIVE DEFENSE—

(1) DEFENSE—It is an affirmative defense to prosecution under this section that the defendant, in good faith, has restricted access by minors to material that is harmful to minors—

(A) by requiring use of a credit card, debit account, adult access code, or adult personal identification number;

(B) by accepting a digital certificate that verifies age; or

(C) by any other reasonable measures that are feasible under available technology.

(2) PROTECTION FOR USE OF DEFENSES—No cause of action may be brought in any court or administrative agency against any person on account of any activity that is not in violation of any law punishable by criminal or civil penalty, and that the person has taken in good faith to implement a defense authorized under this subsection or otherwise to restrict or prevent the transmission of, or access to, a communication specified in this section.

(d) PRIVACY PROTECTION REQUIREMENTS—

(1) DISCLOSURE OF INFORMATION LIMITED—A person making a communication described in subsection (a)—

(A) shall not disclose any information collected for the purposes of restricting access to such communications to individuals 17 years of age or older without the prior written or electronic consent of—

(i) the individual concerned, if the individual is an adult; or

(ii) the individual's parent or guardian, if the individual is under 17 years of age; and

(B) shall take such actions as are necessary to prevent unauthorized access to such information by a person other than the person making such communication and the recipient of such communication.

(2) EXCEPTIONS—A person making a communication described in subsection (a) may disclose such information if the disclosure is—

(A) necessary to make the communication or conduct a legitimate business activity related to making the communication; or

(B) made pursuant to a court order authorizing such disclosure.

(e) DEFINITIONS—For purposes of this subsection, the following definitions shall apply:

(1) BY MEANS OF THE WORLD WIDE WEB—The term 'by means of the World Wide Web' means by placement of material in a computer server-based file archive so that it is publicly accessible, over the Internet, using hypertext transfer protocol or any successor protocol.

(2) COMMERCIAL PURPOSES; ENGAGED IN THE BUSINESS—

(A) COMMERCIAL PURPOSES—A person shall be considered to make a communication for commercial purposes only if such person is engaged in the business of making such communications.

(B) ENGAGED IN THE BUSINESS—The term 'engaged in the business' means that the person who makes a communication, or offers to make a communication, by means of the World Wide Web, that includes any material that is harmful to minors, devotes time, attention, or labor to such activities, as a regular course of such person's trade or business, with the objective of earning a profit as a result of such activities (although it is not necessary that the person make a profit or that the making or offering to make such communications be the person's sole or principal business or source of income). A person may be considered to be engaged in the business of making, by means of the World Wide Web, communications for commercial purposes that include material that is harmful to minors, only if the person knowingly causes the material that is harmful to minors to be posted on the World Wide Web or knowingly solicits such material to be posted on the World Wide Web.

(3) INTERNET—The term 'Internet' means the combination of computer facilities and electromagnetic transmission media, and related equipment and software, comprising the interconnected worldwide net-

work of computer networks that employ the Transmission Control Protocol/Internet Protocol or any successor protocol to transmit information.

(4) INTERNET ACCESS SERVICE—The term 'Internet access service' means a service that enables users to access content, information, electronic mail, or other services offered over the Internet, and may also include access to proprietary content, information, and other services as part of a package of services offered to consumers. Such term does not include telecommunications services.

(5) INTERNET INFORMATION LOCATION TOOL—The term 'Internet information location tool' means a service that refers or links users to an online location on the World Wide Web. Such term includes directories, indices, references, pointers, and hypertext links.

(6) MATERIAL THAT IS HARMFUL TO MINORS—The term 'material that is harmful to minors' means any communication, picture, image, graphic image file, article, recording, writing, or

(A) the average person, applying contemporary community standards, would find, taking the material as a whole and with respect to minors, is designed to appeal to, or is designed to pander to, the prurient interest;

(B) depicts, describes, or represents, in a manner patently offensive with respect to minors, an actual or simulated sexual act or sexual contact, an actual or simulated normal or perverted sexual act, or a lewd exhibition of the genitals or post-pubescent female breast; and

(C) taken as a whole, lacks serious literary, artistic, political, or scientific value for minors.

(7) MINOR—The term 'minor' means any person under 17 years of age.'.

SECTION 103. NOTICE REQUIREMENT.

(a) NOTICE—Section 230 of the Communications Act of 1934 (47 U.S.C. 230) is amended—

(1) in subsection (d)(1), by inserting or 231' after section 223';

(2) by redesignating subsections (d) and (e) as subsections (e) and (f), respectively; and

(3) by inserting after subsection (c) the following new subsection:

(d) OBLIGATIONS OF INTERACTIVE COMPUTER SERV-ICE—A provider of interactive computer service shall, at the time of entering an agreement with a customer for the provision of interactive computer service and in a manner deemed appropriate by the provider, notify such customer that parental control protections (such as computer hardware, software, or filtering services) are commercially available that may assist the customer in limiting access to material that is harmful to minors. Such notice shall identify, or provide the customer with access to information identifying, current providers of such protections.

(b) CONFORMING AMENDMENT—Section 223(h)(2) of the Communications Act of 1934 (47 U.S.C. 223(h)(2)) is amended by striking 230(e)(2)' and inserting 230(f)(2)'.

SECTION 104. STUDY BY COMMISSION ON ONLINE CHILD PROTECTION.

(a) ESTABLISHMENT—There is hereby established a temporary Commission to be known as the Commission on Online Child Protection (in this section referred to as the 'Commission') for the purpose of conducting a study under this section regarding methods to help reduce access by minors to material that is harmful to minors on the Internet.

(b) MEMBERSHIP—The Commission shall be composed of 19 members, as follows:

(1) INDUSTRY MEMBERS—The Commission shall include—

(A) 2 members who are engaged in the business of providing Internet filtering or blocking services or software;

(B) 2 members who are engaged in the business of providing Internet access services;

(C) 2 members who are engaged in the business of providing labeling or ratings services;

(D) 2 members who are engaged in the business of providing Internet portal or search services;

(E) 2 members who are engaged in the business of providing domain name registration services;

(F) 2 members who are academic experts in the field of technology; and

(G) 4 members who are engaged in the business of making content available over the Internet.

Of the members of the Commission by reason of each subparagraph of this paragraph, an equal number shall be appointed by the Speaker of the House of Representatives and by the Majority Leader of the Senate.

(2) EX OFFICIO MEMBERS—The Commission shall include the following officials:

(A) The Assistant Secretary (or the Assistant Secretary's designee).

(B) The Attorney General (or the Attorney General's designee).

(C) The Chairman of the Federal Trade Commission (or the Chairman's designee).

(c) STUDY—

(1) IN GENERAL—The Commission shall conduct a study to identify technological or other methods that—

(A) will help reduce access by minors to material that is harmful to minors on the Internet; and

(B) may meet the requirements for use as affirmative defenses for purposes of section 231(c) of the Communications Act of 1934 (as added by this Act).

Any methods so identified shall be used as the basis for making legislative recommendations to the Congress under subsection (d)(3).

(2) SPECIFIC METHODS—In carrying out the study, the Commission shall identify and analyze various technological tools and methods for protecting minors from material that is harmful to minors, which shall include (without limitation)—

(A) a common resource for parents to use to help protect minors (such as a 'one-click-away' resource);

(B) filtering or blocking software or services;

(C) labeling or rating systems;

(D) age verification systems;

(E) the establishment of a domain name for posting of any material that is harmful to minors; and

(F) any other existing or proposed technologies or methods for reducing access by minors to such material.

(3) ANALYSIS—In analyzing technologies and other methods identified pursuant to paragraph (2), the Commission shall examine—

(A) the cost of such technologies and methods;

(B) the effects of such technologies and methods on law enforcement entities;

(C) the effects of such technologies and methods on privacy;

(D) the extent to which material that is harmful to minors is globally distributed and the effect of such technologies and methods on such distribution;

(E) the accessibility of such technologies and methods to parents; and

(F) such other factors and issues as the Commission considers relevant and appropriate.

(d) REPORT—Not later than 1 year after the enactment of this Act, the Commission shall submit a report to the Congress containing the results of the study under this section, which shall include—

(1) a description of the technologies and methods identified by the study and the results of the analysis of each such technology and method;

(2) the conclusions and recommendations of the Commission regarding each such technology or method;

(3) recommendations for legislative or administrative actions to implement the conclusions of the committee; and

(4) a description of the technologies or methods identified by the study that may meet the requirements for use as affirmative defenses for purposes of section 231(c) of the Communications Act of 1934 (as added by this Act).

(e) STAFF AND RESOURCES—The Assistant Secretary for Communication and Information of the Department of Commerce shall provide to the Commission such staff and resources as the Assistant Secretary determines necessary for the Commission to perform its duty efficiently and in accordance with this section.

(f) TERMINATION—The Commission shall terminate 30 days after the submission of the report under subsection (d).

(g) INAPPLICABILITY OF FEDERAL ADVISORY COMMITTEE ACT—The Federal Advisory Committee Act (5 U.S.C. App.) shall not apply to the Commission.

SECTION 105. EFFECTIVE DATE.

This title and the amendments made by this title shall take effect 30 days after the date of enactment of this Act.

TITLE II—CHILDREN'S ONLINE PRIVACY PROTECTION

SECTION 201. DEFINITIONS.

In this title:

(1) CHILD—The term child' means an individual under the age of 13.

(2) OPERATOR—The term operator' means any person operating a website on the World Wide Web or any online service for commercial purposes, including any person offering products or services for sale through that website or online service, involving commerce—

(A) among the several States or with 1 or more foreign nations;

(B) in any territory of the United States or in the District of Columbia, or between any such territory and—

(i) another such territory; or

(ii) any State or foreign nation; or

(C) between the District of Columbia and any State, territory, or foreign nation.

For purposes of this title, the term 'operator' does not include any non-profit entity that would otherwise be exempt from coverage under section 5 of the Federal Trade Commission Act (15 U.S.C. 45).

(3) COMMISSION—The term Commission' means the Federal Trade Commission.

(4) DISCLOSURE—The term disclosure' means, with respect to personal information—

(A) the release of personal information collected from a child in identifiable form by an operator for any purpose, except where such information is provided to a person other than the operator who provides support for the internal operations of the website and does not disclose or use that information for any other purpose; and

(B) making personal information collected from a child by a website or online service directed to children or with actual knowledge that such information was collected from a child, publicly available in identifiable form, by any means including by a public posting, through the Internet, or through—-

(i) a home page of a website;

(ii) a pen pal service;

(iii) an electronic mail service;

(iv) a message board; or

(v) a chat room.

(5) FEDERAL AGENCY—The term Federal agency' means an agency, as that term is defined in section 551(1) of title 5, United States Code.

(6) INTERNET—The term Internet' means collectively the myriad of computer and telecommunications facilities, including equipment and operating software, which comprise the interconnected world-wide network of networks that employ the Transmission Control Protocol/Internet Protocol, or any predecessor or successor protocols to such protocol, to communicate information of all kinds by wire or radio.

(7) PARENT—The term parent' includes a legal guardian.

(8) PERSONAL INFORMATION—The term personal information' means individually identifiable information about an individual collected online, including—

(A) a first and last name;

(B) a home or other physical address including street name and name of a city or town;

(C) an e-mail address;

(D) a telephone number;

(E) a Social Security number;

(F) any other identifier that the Commission determines permits the physical or online contacting of a specific individual; or

(G) information concerning the child or the parents of that child that the website collects online from the child and combines with an identifier described in this paragraph.

(9) VERIFIABLE PARENTAL CONSENT—The term verifiable parental consent' means any reasonable effort (taking into consideration available technology), including a request for authorization for future collection, use, and disclosure described in the notice, to ensure that a parent of a child receives notice of the operator's personal information

collection, use, and disclosure practices, and authorizes the collection, use, and disclosure, as applicable, of personal information and the subsequent use of that information before that information is collected from that child.

(10) WEBSITE OR ONLINE SERVICE DIRECTED TO CHILDREN—

(A) IN GENERAL—The term website or online service directed to children' means —

(i) a commercial website or online service that is targeted to children; or

(ii) that portion of a commercial website or online service that is targeted to children.

(B) LIMITATION—A commercial website or online service, or a portion of a commercial website or online service, shall not be deemed directed to children solely for referring or linking to a commercial website or online service directed to children by using information location tools, including a directory, index, reference, pointer, or hypertext link.

(11) PERSON—The term person' means any individual, partnership, corporation, trust, estate, cooperative, association, or other entity.

(12) ONLINE CONTACT INFORMATION—The term online contact information' means an e-mail address or another substantially similar identifier that permits direct contact with a person online.

SECTION 202. REGULATION OF UNFAIR AND DECEPTIVE ACTS AND PRACTICES IN CONNECTION WITH THE COLLECTION AND USE OF PERSONAL INFORMATION FROM AND ABOUT CHILDREN ON THE INTERNET.

(a) ACTS PROHIBITED—

(1) IN GENERAL—It is unlawful for an operator of a website or online service directed to children, or any operator that has actual knowledge that it is collecting personal information from a child, to collect personal information from a child in a manner that violates the regulations prescribed under subsection (b).

(2) DISCLOSURE TO PARENT PROTECTED—Notwithstanding paragraph (1), neither an operator of such a website or online service nor the operator's agent shall be held to be liable under any Federal or State

law for any disclosure made in good faith and following reasonable procedures in responding to a request for disclosure of personal information under subsection (b)(1)(B)(iii) to the parent of a child.

(b) REGULATIONS—

(1) IN GENERAL—Not later than 1 year after the date of the enactment of this Act, the Commission shall promulgate under section 553 of title 5, United States Code, regulations that—

(A) require the operator of any website or online service directed to children that collects personal information from children or the operator of a website or online service that has actual knowledge that it is collecting personal information from a child—

(i) to provide notice on the website of what information is collected from children by the operator, how the operator uses such information, and the operator's disclosure practices for such information; and

(ii) to obtain verifiable parental consent for the collection, use, or disclosure of personal information from children;

(B) require the operator to provide, upon request of a parent whose child has provided personal information to that website or online service—

(i) a description of the specific types of personal information collected from the child by that operator;

(ii) notwithstanding any other provision of law, the opportunity at any time to refuse to permit the operator's further use or maintenance in retrievable form, or future online collection, of personal information on that child; and

(iii) a means that is reasonable under the circumstances for the parent to obtain any personal information collected from that child;

(C) prohibit conditioning a child's participation in a game, the offering of a prize, or another activity on the child disclosing more personal information than is reasonably necessary to participate in such activity;

(D) require the operator of such a website or online service to establish and maintain reasonable procedures to protect the confidentiality, security, and integrity of personal information collected from children; and

(E) permit the operator of such a website or online service to collect, use, and disseminate such information as is necessary—

   (i) to protect the security or integrity of its website;

   (ii) to take precautions against liability;

   (iii) to respond to judicial process; and

   (iv) to provide information to law enforcement agencies or for an investigation on a matter related to public safety.

(2) WHEN CONSENT NOT REQUIRED—Verifiable parental consent under paragraph (1)(A)(ii) is not required in the case of—

(A) online contact information collected from a child that is used only to respond directly on a one-time basis to a specific request from the child and is not used to recontact the child and is not maintained in retrievable form by the operator;

(B) a request for the name or online contact information of a parent or child that is used for the sole purpose of obtaining parental consent or providing notice under this section and where such information is not maintained in retrievable form by the operator if parental consent is not obtained after a reasonable time;

(C) online contact information collected from a child that is used only to respond more than once directly to a specific request from the child and is not used to recontact the child beyond the scope of that request—

   (i) if, before any additional response after the initial response to the child, the operator uses reasonable efforts to provide a parent notice of the online contact information collected from the child, the purposes for which it is to be used, and an opportunity for the parent to request that the operator make no further use of the information and that it not be maintained in retrievable form; or

   (ii) without notice to the parent in such circumstances as the Commission may determine are appropriate, taking into consideration the benefits to the child of access to information and services, and risks to the security and privacy of the child, in regulations promulgated under this subsection; or

(D) the name of the child and online contact information (to the extent necessary to protect the safety of a child participant in the site)—

   (i) used only for the purpose of protecting such safety;

(ii) not used to recontact the child or for any other purpose; and

(iii) not disclosed on the site,

if the operator uses reasonable efforts to provide a parent notice of the name and online contact information collected from the child, the purposes for which it is to be used, and an opportunity for the parent to request that the operator make no further use of the information and that it not be maintained in retrievable form.

(c) ENFORCEMENT—Subject to sections 203 and 205, a violation of a regulation prescribed under subsection (a) shall be treated as a violation of a rule defining an unfair or deceptive act or practice prescribed under section 18(a)(1)(B) of the Federal Trade Commission Act (15 U.S.C. 57a(a)(1)(B)).

(d) INCONSISTENT STATE LAW—No State or local government may impose any liability for commercial activities or actions by operators in interstate or foreign commerce in connection with an activity or action described in this title that is inconsistent with the treatment of those activities or actions under this section.

SECTION 203. SAFE HARBORS.

(a) GUIDELINES—An operator may satisfy the requirements of regulations issued under section 202(b) by following a set of self-regulatory guidelines, issued by representatives of the marketing or online industries, or by other persons, approved under subsection (b).

(b) INCENTIVES—

(1) SELF-REGULATORY INCENTIVES—In prescribing regulations under section 202, the Commission shall provide incentives for self-regulation by operators to implement the protections afforded children under the regulatory requirements described in subsection (b) of that section.

(2) DEEMED COMPLIANCE—Such incentives shall include provisions for ensuring that a person will be deemed to be in compliance with the requirements of the regulations under section 202 if that person complies with guidelines that, after notice and comment, are approved by the Commission upon making a determination that the guidelines meet the requirements of the regulations issued under section 202.

(3) EXPEDITED RESPONSE TO REQUESTS—The Commission shall act upon requests for safe harbor treatment within 180 days of the filing

of the request, and shall set forth in writing its conclusions with regard to such requests.

(c) APPEALS—Final action by the Commission on a request for approval of guidelines, or the failure to act within 180 days on a request for approval of guidelines, submitted under subsection (b) may be appealed to a district court of the United States of appropriate jurisdiction as provided for in section 706 of title 5, United States Code.

SECTION 204. ACTIONS BY STATES.

(a) IN GENERAL—

(1) CIVIL ACTIONS—In any case in which the attorney general of a State has reason to believe that an interest of the residents of that State has been or is threatened or adversely affected by the engagement of any person in a practice that violates any regulation of the Commission prescribed under section 202(b), the State, as parens patriae, may bring a civil action on behalf of the residents of the State in a district court of the United States of appropriate jurisdiction to—

(A) enjoin that practice;

(B) enforce compliance with the regulation;

(C) obtain damage, restitution, or other compensation on behalf of residents of the State; or

(D) obtain such other relief as the court may consider to be appropriate.

(2) NOTICE-

(A) IN GENERAL—Before filing an action under paragraph (1), the attorney general of the State involved shall provide to the Commission—

(i) written notice of that action; and

(ii) a copy of the complaint for that action.

(B) EXEMPTION—

(i) IN GENERAL—Subparagraph (A) shall not apply with respect to the filing of an action by an attorney general of a State under this subsection, if the attorney general determines that it is not feasible to provide the notice described in that subparagraph before the filing of the action.

(ii) NOTIFICATION—In an action described in clause (i), the attorney general of a State shall provide notice and a copy of the complaint to the Commission at the same time as the attorney general files the action.

(b) INTERVENTION—

(1) IN GENERAL—On receiving notice under subsection (a)(2), the Commission shall have the right to intervene in the action that is the subject of the notice.

(2) EFFECT OF INTERVENTION—If the Commission intervenes in an action under subsection(a), it shall have the right—

(A) to be heard with respect to any matter that arises in that action; and

(B) to file a petition for appeal.

(3) AMICUS CURIAE—Upon application to the court, a person whose self-regulatory guidelines have been approved by the Commission and are relied upon as a defense by any defendant to a proceeding under this section may file amicus curiae in that proceeding.

(c) CONSTRUCTION—For purposes of bringing any civil action under subsection (a), nothing in this title shall be construed to prevent an attorney general of a State from exercising the powers conferred on the attorney general by the laws of that State to—

(1) conduct investigations;

(2) administer oaths or affirmations; or

(3) compel the attendance of witnesses or the production of documentary and other evidence.

(d) ACTIONS BY THE COMMISSION—In any case in which an action is instituted by or on behalf of the Commission for violation of any regulation prescribed under section 202, no State may, during the pendency of that action, institute an action under subsection (a) against any defendant named in the complaint in that action for violation of that regulation.

(e) VENUE; SERVICE OF PROCESS—

(1) VENUE—Any action brought under subsection (a) may be brought in the district court of the United States that meets applicable requirements relating to venue under section 1391 of title 28, United States Code.

(2) SERVICE OF PROCESS—In an action brought under subsection (a), process may be served in any district in which the defendant—

(A) is an inhabitant; or

(B) may be found.

SECTION 205. ADMINISTRATION AND APPLICABILITY OF ACT.

(a) IN GENERAL—Except as otherwise provided, this title shall be enforced by the Commission under the Federal Trade Commission Act (15 U.S.C. 41 et seq.).

(b) PROVISIONS—Compliance with the requirements imposed under this title shall be enforced under—

(1) section 8 of the Federal Deposit Insurance Act (12 U.S.C. 1818), in the case of—

(A) national banks, and Federal branches and Federal agencies of foreign banks, by the Office of the Comptroller of the Currency;

(B) member banks of the Federal Reserve System (other than national banks), branches and agencies of foreign banks (other than Federal branches, Federal agencies, and insured State branches of foreign banks), commercial lending companies owned or controlled by foreign banks, and organizations operating under section 25 or 25(a) of the Federal Reserve Act (12 U.S.C. 601 et seq. and 611 et. seq.), by the Board; and

(C) banks insured by the Federal Deposit Insurance Corporation (other than members of the Federal Reserve System) and insured State branches of foreign banks, by the Board of Directors of the Federal Deposit Insurance Corporation;

(2) section 8 of the Federal Deposit Insurance Act (12 U.S.C. 1818), by the Director of the Office of Thrift Supervision, in the case of a savings association the deposits of which are insured by the Federal Deposit Insurance Corporation;

(3) the Federal Credit Union Act (12 U.S.C. 1751 et seq.) by the National Credit Union Administration Board with respect to any Federal credit union;

(4) part A of subtitle VII of title 49, United States Code, by the Secretary of Transportation with respect to any air carrier or foreign air carrier subject to that part;

(5) the Packers and Stockyards Act, 1921 (7 U.S.C. 181 et. seq.) (except as provided in section 406 of that Act (7 U.S.C. 226, 227)), by the Secretary of Agriculture with respect to any activities subject to that Act; and

(6) the Farm Credit Act of 1971 (12 U.S.C. (2001 et seq.) by the Farm Credit Administration with respect to any Federal land bank, Federal land bank association, Federal intermediate credit bank, or production credit association.

(c) EXERCISE OF CERTAIN POWERS—For the purpose of the exercise by any agency referred to in subsection (a) of its powers under any Act referred to in that subsection, a violation of any requirement imposed under this title shall be deemed to be a violation of a requirement imposed under that Act. In addition to its powers under any provision of law specifically referred to in subsection (a), each of the agencies referred to in that subsection may exercise, for the purpose of enforcing compliance with any requirement imposed under this title, any other authority conferred on it by law.

(d) ACTIONS BY THE COMMISSION—The Commission shall prevent any person from violating a rule of the Commission under section 202 in the same manner, by the same means, and with the same jurisdiction, powers, and duties as though all applicable terms and provisions of the Federal Trade Commission Act (15 U.S.C. 41 et seq.) were incorporated into and made a part of this title. Any entity that violates such rule shall be subject to the penalties and entitled to the privileges and immunities provided in the Federal Trade Commission Act in the same manner, by the same means, and with the same jurisdiction, power, and duties as though all applicable terms and provisions of the Federal Trade Commission Act were incorporated into and made a part of this title.

(e) EFFECT ON OTHER LAWS—Nothing contained in this title shall be construed to limit the authority of the Commission under any other provisions of law.

SECTION 206. REVIEW.

Not later than 5 years after the effective date of the regulations initially issued under section 202, the Commission shall—

(1) review the implementation of this title, including the effect of the implementation of this title on practices relating to the collection and disclosure of information relating to children, children's ability to obtain access to information of their choice online, and on the availability of websites directed to children; and

(2) prepare and submit to Congress a report on the results of the review under paragraph (1).

SECTION 207. EFFECTIVE DATE.

Sections 202(a), 204, and 205 of this title take effect on the later of—

(1) the date that is 18 months after the date of enactment of this Act; or

(2) the date on which the Commission rules on the first application for safe harbor treatment under section 203 if the Commission does not rule on the first such application within one year after the date of enactment of this Act, but in no case later than the date that is 30 months after the date of enactment of this Act.

Passed the House of Representatives October 7, 1998.

APPENDIX 9:

THE SAFE SCHOOLS INTERNET ACT OF 1999

SECTION 1. SHORT TITLE.

This Act may be cited as the "Safe Schools Internet Act of 1999."

SECTION 2. NO UNIVERSAL SERVICE FOR SCHOOLS OR LIBRARIES THAT FAIL TO IMPLEMENT A FILTERING OR BLOCKING SYSTEM FOR COMPUTERS WITH INTERNET ACCESS.

(a) IN GENERAL—Section 254 of the Communications Act of 1934 (47 U.S.C. 254) is amended by adding at the end thereof the following:

(l) IMPLEMENTATION OF A FILTERING OR BLOCKING SYSTEM—

(1) IN GENERAL—No services may be provided under subsection (h)(1)(B) to any elementary or secondary school , or any library, unless it provides the certification required by paragraph (2) or (3), respectively.

(2) CERTIFICATION FOR SCHOOLS —Before receiving universal service assistance under subsection (h)(1)(B), an elementary or secondary school (or the school board or other authority with responsibility for administration of that school) shall certify to the Commission that it has—

(A) selected a system for computers with Internet access to filter or block matter deemed to be inappropriate for minors; and

(B) installed, or will install as soon as it obtains computers with Internet access, a system to filter or block such matter.

(3) CERTIFICATION FOR LIBRARIES—Before receiving universal service assistance under subsection (h)(1)(B), a library that has a computer with Internet access shall certify to the Commission that, on one or more of its computers with Internet access, it employs a system to filter or block matter deemed to be inappropriate for minors. If a library that makes a certification under this paragraph changes the system it employs or ceases to employ any such system, it shall notify the Commission within 10 days after implementing the change or ceasing to employ the system.

(4) LOCAL DETERMINATION OF CONTENT—For purposes of paragraphs (2) and (3), the determination of what matter is inappropriate for minors shall be made by the school , school board, library or other authority responsible for making the required certification. No agency or instrumentality of the United States Government may—

(A) establish criteria for making that determination;

(B) review the determination made by the certifying school, school board, library, or other authority; or

(C) consider the criteria employed by the certifying school, school board, library, or other authority in the administration of subsection (h)(1)(B).

(b) CONFORMING CHANGE —Section 254(h)(1)(B) of the Communications Act of 1934 (47 U.S.C. 254(h)(1)(B)) is amended by striking All telecommunications' and inserting Except as provided by subsection (l), all telecommunications'.

THE HATE CRIMES PREVENTION ACT OF 1999

SECTION 1. SHORT TITLE.

This Act may be cited as the Hate Crimes Prevention Act of 1999'.

SECTION 2. FINDINGS.

Congress finds that—

(1) the incidence of violence motivated by the actual or perceived race, color, national origin, religion, sexual orientation, gender, or disability of the victim poses a serious national problem;

(2) such violence disrupts the tranquility and safety of communities and is deeply divisive;

(3) existing Federal law is inadequate to address this problem;

(4) such violence affects interstate commerce in many ways, including—

(A) by impeding the movement of members of targeted groups and forcing such members to move across State lines to escape the incidence or risk of such violence; and

(B) by preventing members of targeted groups from purchasing goods and services, obtaining or sustaining employment or participating in other commercial activity;

(5) perpetrators cross State lines to commit such violence;

(6) instrumentalities of interstate commerce are used to facilitate the commission of such violence;

(7) such violence is committed using articles that have traveled in interstate commerce;

(8) violence motivated by bias that is a relic of slavery can constitute badges and incidents of slavery;

(9) although many State and local authorities are now and will continue to be responsible for prosecuting the overwhelming majority of violent crimes in the United States, including violent crimes motivated by bias, Federal jurisdiction over certain violent crimes motivated by bias is necessary to supplement State and local jurisdiction and ensure that justice is achieved in each case;

(10) Federal jurisdiction over certain violent crimes motivated by bias enables Federal, State, and local authorities to work together as partners in the investigation and prosecution of such crimes ; and

(11) the problem of hate crime is sufficiently serious, widespread, and interstate in nature as to warrant Federal assistance to States and local jurisdictions.

SECTION 3. DEFINITION OF HATE CRIME.

In this Act, the term 'hate crime' has the same meaning as in section 280003(a) of the Violent Crime Control and Law Enforcement Act of 1994 (28 U.S.C. 994 note).

SECTION 4. PROHIBITION OF CERTAIN ACTS OF VIOLENCE.

Section 245 of title 18, United States Code, is amended—

(1) by redesignating subsections (c) and (d) as subsections (d) and (e), respectively; and

(2) by inserting after subsection (b) the following:

(c)(1) Whoever, whether or not acting under color of law, willfully causes bodily injury to any person or, through the use of fire, a firearm, or an explosive device, attempts to cause bodily injury to any person, because of the actual or perceived race, color, religion, or national origin of any person—

(A) shall be imprisoned not more than 10 years, or fined in accordance with this title, or both; and

(B) shall be imprisoned for any term of years or for life, or fined in accordance with this title, or both if—

(i) death results from the acts committed in violation of this paragraph; or

(ii) the acts omitted in violation of this paragraph include kidnapping or an attempt to kidnap, aggravated sexual abuse or an attempt to commit aggravated sexual abuse, or an attempt to kill.

(2)(A) Whoever, whether or not acting under color of law, in any circumstance described in subparagraph (B), willfully causes bodily injury to any person or, through the use of fire, a firearm, or an explosive device, attempts to cause bodily injury to any person, because of the actual or perceived religion, gender, sexual orientation, or disability of any person—-

(i) shall be imprisoned not more than 10 years, or fined in accordance with this title, or both; and

(ii) shall be imprisoned for any term of years or for life, or fined in accordance with this title, or both, if—

(I) death results from the acts committed in violation of this paragraph; or

(II) the acts committed in violation of this paragraph include kidnapping or an attempt to kidnap, aggravated sexual abuse or an attempt to commit aggravated sexual abuse, or an attempt to kill.

(B) For purposes of subparagraph (A), the circumstances described in this subparagraph are that—

(i) in connection with the offense, the defendant or the victim travels in interstate or foreign commerce, uses a facility or instrumentality of interstate or foreign commerce, or engages in any activity affecting interstate or foreign commerce; or

(ii) the offense is in or affects interstate or foreign commerce.'.

SECTION 5. DUTIES OF FEDERAL SENTENCING COMMISSION.

(a) AMENDMENT OF FEDERAL SENTENCING GUIDELINES—Pursuant to its authority under section 994 of title 28, United States Code, the United States Sentencing Commission shall study the issue of adult recruitment of juveniles to commit hate crimes and shall, if appropriate, amend the Federal sentencing guidelines to provide sentencing enhancements (in addition to the sentencing enhancement provided for the use of a minor during the commission of an offense) for adult defendants who recruit juveniles to assist in the commission of hate crimes .

(b) CONSISTENCY WITH OTHER GUIDELINES—In carrying out this section, the United States Sentencing Commission shall—

(1) ensure that there is reasonable consistency with other Federal sentencing guidelines; and

(2) avoid duplicative punishments for substantially the same offense.

SECTION 6. GRANT PROGRAM.

(a) AUTHORITY TO MAKE GRANTS—The Office of Justice Programs of the Department of Justice shall make grants, in accordance with such regulations as the Attorney General may prescribe, to State and local programs designed to combat hate crimes committed by juveniles, including programs to train local law enforcement officers in investigating, prosecuting, and preventing hate crimes .

(b) AUTHORIZATION OF APPROPRIATIONS—There are authorized to be appropriated such sums as may be necessary to carry out this section.

SECTION 7. AUTHORIZATION FOR ADDITIONAL PERSONNEL TO ASSIST STATE AND LOCAL LAW ENFORCEMENT.

There are authorized to be appropriated to the Department of the Treasury and the Department of Justice, including the Community Relations Service, for fiscal years 1998, 1999, and 2000 such sums as are necessary to increase the number of personnel to prevent and respond to alleged violations of section 245 of title 18, United States Code (as amended by this Act).

SECTION 8. SEVERABILITY.

If any provision of this Act, an amendment made by this Act, or the application of such provision or amendment to any person or circumstance is held to be unconstitutional, the remainder of this Act, the amendments made by this Act, and the application of the provisions of such to any person or circumstance shall not be affected thereby.

GLOSSARY

GLOSSARY

Abolish - To repeal or revoke, such as a law or custom.

Abrogate - To annul, destroy, revoke, or cancel; the legislative repeal of a law.

Abstention - A policy adopted by the federal courts whereby the district court may decline to exercise its jurisdiction and defer to a state court the resolution of a federal constitutional question, pending the outcome in a state court proceeding.

Abuse of Discretion - A standard of review.

Acquit - A verdict of "not guilty" which determines that the person is absolved of the charge and prevents a retrial pursuant to the doctrine of double jeopardy.

Acquittal - One who is acquitted receives an acquittal, which is a release without further prosecution.

American Civil Liberties Union (ACLU) - A nationwide organization dedicated to the enforcement and preservation of rights and civil liberties guaranteed by the federal and state constitutions.

Appeal - Resort to a higher court for the purpose of obtaining a review of a lower court decision.

Appellate Court - A court having jurisdiction to review the law as applied to a prior determination of the same case.

Argument - A discourse set forth for the purpose of establishing one's position in a controversy.

Arrest - To deprive a person of his liberty by legal authority.

Bill of Rights - The first eight amendments to the United States Constitution.

Blacklisting - The act of excluding qualified persons from employment or other responsibilities on the basis of their political opinions or associations.

Bowdlerize - The process of expurgating and revising literary works in order to remove objectionable language or ideas.

Chief Justice - The presiding member of certain courts which have more than one judge, e.g., the United States Supreme Court.

Circuit - A judicial division of a state or the United States.

Circuit Court - One of several courts in a given jurisdiction.

Civil Disobedience - The refusal to obey a law for the purpose of demonstrating its unfairness.

Civil Disorder - A violent public disturbance involving a group of three or more persons, which causes immediate danger, damage or injury to the property or person of another.

Civil Law - Law which applies to noncriminal actions.

Common Law - Common law is the system of jurisprudence which originated in England and was later applied in the United States.

Conspiracy - A scheme by two or more persons to commit a criminal or unlawful act.

Conspirator - One of the parties involved in a conspiracy.

Constitution - The fundamental principles of law which frame a governmental system.

Constitutional Right - Refers to the individual liberties granted by the constitution of a state or the federal government.

Court - The branch of government responsible for the resolution of disputes arising under the laws of the government.

Court of Claims - The federal court created to resolve claims against the United States.

Criminal Syndicalism - Type of statute which prohibits and punishes anarchism, the violent overthrow of the government and other forms of rebellions or revolution.

Defamation - A form of unprotected speech that occurs upon publication of an injurious statement, either written or oral, about the reputation, character, integrity or morality of another.

Due Process Rights - All rights which are of such fundamental importance as to require compliance with due process standards of fairness and justice.

Fairness Doctrine - An FCC regulation requiring radio and television broadcasters to provide coverage of issues of public importance and to present contrasting views.

Federal Courts - The courts of the United States.

The First Amendment - The First Amendment of the United States Constitution protects the right to freedom of religion and freedom of expression from government interference.

Flag Desecration - The burning or other desecration of the United States flag as a form of political expression.

Freedom of Information Act (FOIA) - A federal law which requires federal agencies to disclose information in its possession which is not exempt from the law.

Gag Order - An order imposed by the court restricting comment about a case.

Hate Speech - A term used to describe speech that attacks individuals or groups on the basis of their race, ethnicity, religion or sexual orientation.

Indecency - Expression that is morally indelicate, improper, offensive or tending to be obscene.

Indictment - A formal written accusation of criminal charges submitted to a grand jury for investigation and indorsement.

Injunction - A judicial remedy either requiring a party to perform an act, or restricting a party from continuing a particular act.

Injury - Any damage done to another's person, rights, reputation or property.

Internet - A worldwide system of linked computer networks.

Judge - The individual who presides over a court, and whose function it is to determine controversies.

Labor Organization - An association of workers for the purpose of bargaining the terms and conditions of employment on behalf of labor and management.

Libel - A form of unprotected speech involving the false and malicious publication of defamatory words that are written or broadcast.

Malice - A state of mind that accompanies the intentional commission of a wrongful act.

National Labor Relations Board - An independent agency created by the National Labor Relations Act of 1935 (Wagner Act), as amended by the acts of 1947 (Taft-Hartley Act) and 1959 (Landrum-Griffin Act), established to regulate the relations between employers and employees.

Oath - A sworn declaration of the truth under penalty of perjury.

Obscene Material - Material which lacks serious literary, artistic, political or scientific value and, taken as a whole, appeals to the prurient interest and, as such, is not protected by the free speech guarantee of the First Amendment.

Opinion - The reasoning behind a court's decision.

Ordinance - A local law passed by a municipal legislative body.

Overrule - A holding in a particular case is overruled when the same court, or a higher court, in that jurisdiction, makes an opposite ruling in a subsequent case on the identical point of law ruled upon in the prior case.

The Pentagon Papers - A classified Pentagon study of the history of the United States involvement in Vietnam.

Petitioner - One who presents a petition to a court or other body either in order to institute an equity proceeding or to take an appeal from a judgment.

Police Power - The power of the state to restrict private individuals in matters relating to public health, safety, and morality, and to impose such other restrictions as may be necessary to promote the welfare of the general public.

Precedent - A previously decided case which is recognized as authority for the disposition of future cases.

Prima Facie Case - A case which is sufficient on its face, being supported by at least the requisite minimum of evidence, and being free from palpable defects.

Prior Restraint - Legal action taken to suppress speech prior to its expression rather than punishing it on the basis of what was said.

Prosecution - The process of pursuing a civil lawsuit or a criminal trial.

Prosecutor - The individual who prepares a criminal case against an individual accused of a crime.

Prurient Interest - The shameful and morbid interest in nudity and sex.

Question of Law - The question of law which is the province of the judge to decide.

Racketeering - An organized conspiracy to commit extortion.

Rational Basis Test - The constitutional analysis of a law to determine whether it has a reasonable relationship to some legitimate government objective so as to uphold the law.

Sanction - A form of punishment.

Sedition - An illegal act which tends to cause disruption of the government, short of insurrection.

Sentence - The punishment given a convicted criminal by the court.

Shield Laws - State laws enacted to protect the confidentiality of journalists' sources from legislative, judicial or other official interrogation.

Slander - Spoken words that are damaging to the reputation of another.

Supreme Court - In most jurisdictions, the Supreme Court is the highest appellate court, including the federal court system.

Unconstitutional - Refers to a statute which conflicts with the United States Constitution rendering it void.

Vacate - To render something void, such as a judgment.

V-Chip - A microchip designed to be installed in television sets for the specific purpose of allow parents to screen out undesirable programming.

BIBLIOGRAPHY

BIBLIOGRAPHY

The American Civil Liberties Union. (Date Visited: May 1999) http://www.aclu.org.

The American Library Association. (Date Visited: May 1999) ttp://www.ala.org

Black's Law Dictionary, Fifth Edition. St. Paul, MN: West Publishing Company, 1979.

Cornell Law School Legal Information Institute. (Date Visited: May 1999) http://www.law.cornell.edu/.

The First Amendment Center. (Date Visited: May 1999) http://www.freedomforum.org/first/welcome.asp/.

The First Amendment Project. (Date Visited: May 1999) http://www.thefirstamendment.org.

Foerstel, Herbert N. *Free Expression and Censorship in* America: An Encyclopedia. Westport, CT: Greenwood Press, 1997.

The Free Expression Network. (Date Visited: May 1999) http://www.freeexpression.org.

Godwin, Mike *Cyber Rights: Defending Free Speech in* the Digital Age. New York, NY: Random House, Inc., 1998.

The National Campaign for Freedom of Expression. (Date Visited: May 1999) http://www.ncfe.net.

The National Coalition Against Censorship. (Date Visited: May 1999) http://www.ncac.org.